L

RUSSIAN COURSEBOOK

REVISED & UPDATED

Call auout #
1 800 359 1200
order# 29472576

RUSSIAN COURSEBOOK

REVISED & UPDATED

REVISED BY NADYA L. PETERSON, PH.D.
Assistant Professor of Russian
University of Pennsylvania

◆

Based on the original
by Aron Pressman

LIVING LANGUAGE®
A Random House Company

This work was previously published under the titles *Conversation Manual Russian* and *Living Language™ Conversational Russian* by Aron Pressman.

Copyright © 1993, 1958 by Living Language, A Random House Company

All rights reserved under Pan-American Copyright Conventions. No part of this book may be reproduced or transmitted in any form or by any means, electronic or mechanical, including photocopying, recording, or by any information storage and retrieval system, without permission in writing from the publisher.

Published by Living Language®, A Random House Company, New York, New York.

Random House, Inc., New York, Toronto, London, Sydney, Auckland

www.livinglanguage.com

LIVING LANGUAGE and colophon are registered trademarks of Random House, Inc.

If you're traveling, we recommend **Fodor's guides.**

This book is available for special discounts for bulk purchases for sales promotions or premiums. Special editions, including personalized covers, excerpts of existing books, and corporate imprints, can be created in large quantities for special needs. For more information, write to Special Markets/Premium Sales, 1745 Broadway, MD 6-2, New York, NY, 10019 or e-mail specialmarkets@randomhouse.com.

Printed in the United States of America

ISBN 1-4000-2028-X

10 9 8 7 6

CONTENTS

INTRODUCTION	xiii
COURSE MATERIAL	xiv
INSTRUCTIONS	xv
LESSON 1	1
A. The Letters and Sounds of the Russian Language	1
B. Names	2
C. Geographical Names	4
LESSON 2	6
A. Cognates: Words Similar in Russian and English	6
B. Geographical Names II	8
LESSON 3	9
A. Introduction to the Russian Alphabet	9
B. The Alphabet	9
LESSON 4	11
A. Palatalized and Nonpalatalized Syllables	11

Lesson 5 12
A. Vowels 12

Lesson 6 18
A. Consonants 18

Lesson 7 24
A. Consonants II 24

Lesson 8 29
A. Masculine, Feminine, Neuter, Plural 29
Quiz 1 31

Lesson 9 32
A. Characteristics of the Cases 32
B. Word Study 34

Lesson 10 34
A. Кто? (Who?) and Никто́/Не́кто (No One/Someone) 34
Quiz 2 36
B. Что? (What?) and Ничего́/Не́чего (Nothing) 37
C. Declensions of Nouns, Adjectives, and Pronouns 39
Quiz 3 46

Lesson 11 47
A. Numbers 1–10 47
B. Days and Months 47
C. Seasons and Directions 48
D. Word Study 48

Lesson 12 49
A. Greetings 49
B. Last Month, Last Year, etc. 50
Quiz 4 51

B. The Imperative Mood 171
C. Even More on Perfective and Imperfective Verbs 172
D. Word Study 173
Quiz 26 173

Lesson 38 175
A. Buying Gifts 175
B. Use of the Particles To and Нибудь 178
Quiz 27 178

Lesson 39 180
A. Two Colleagues 180
B. At the Museum 182

Lesson 40 184
A. Problems of the Planet 184
B. Participles and Gerunds 185
Final Review 187

Summary of Russian Grammar 190
1. The Russian Alphabet 190
2. Pronunciation 191
Vowels 191
Consonants 192
3. Gender 193
4. Cases 194
5. Declension of Nouns 196
6. Declension of Adjectives 198
7. Declension of Pronouns 199
8. Comparative of Adjectives 203
9. Superlative of Adjectives 204
10. Cases Used with Cardinal Numerals 204
11. Declension of Cardinal Numerals 205
12. Ordinal Numerals 206
13. Double Negatives 207

14. Verbs 208
A. Typical Conjugations of Imperfective Verbs 208
B. Mixed Conjugation—Present Tense 210
C. Reflexive Verbs 211
D. The Verb "To Be" 211
E. Conjugations of Some Irregular Verbs in the Present Tense 212
F. Conjugations of Irregular Perfective Verbs—Perfective Future 213
G. Perfective and Imperfective Aspects of a Verb 213
H. Future Tense 215
I. Verbs of Motion 216
J. Subjunctive and Conditional Moods 220
K. Imperative Mood 221
L. Participles and Gerunds 222

LETTER WRITING 224
A. A Note on Letter Writing 224
B. Business Letters 225
C. Informal Letters 227
D. Form of the Envelope 229

INTRODUCTION

Living Language® Russian makes it easy to learn how to speak, read, and write Russian. This course is a thoroughly revised and updated version of *Living Russian, The Complete Living Language Course®*. The same highly effective method of language instruction is still used, but the content has been updated to reflect modern usage, and the format has been clarified. In this course, the basic elements of the language have been carefully selected and condensed into forty short lessons. If you can study about thirty minutes a day, you can master this course and learn to speak Russian in a few weeks.

You'll learn Russian the way you learned English, starting with simple words and progressing to more complex phrases. Just listen and repeat after the native instructors on the recordings. To help you immerse yourself in the language, you'll hear only Russian spoken. Hear it, say it, and absorb it through use and repetition.

This *Living Language® Russian Coursebook* provides English translations and brief explanations for each lesson. The first seven lessons cover pronunciation, laying the foundation for learning the vocabulary, phrases, and grammar, which are explained in the later chapters. If you already know a little Russian, you can use the book as a phrase book and reference. In addition to the forty lessons, there is a Summary of Russian Grammar, plus verb conjugations and a section on writing letters.

Also included in the course package is the *Living Language® Russian Dictionary.* It contains more than 15,000 entries, with many of the definitions illustrated by phrases and idiomatic expressions. The most essential words are preceded by an * to make them easy to find. You can increase your vocabulary and range of expression just by browsing through the dictionary.

Practice your Russian as much as possible. Even if you can't manage a trip abroad, watching Russian movies, reading Russian magazines, eating at Russian restaurants, and talking with Russian-speaking friends are enjoyable ways to help reinforce what you have learned with *Living Language® Russian.* Now, let's begin.

The following instructions will tell you what to do. Ни пу́ха, ни пера́! Good luck!

COURSE MATERIAL

1. Two 90-minute cassettes or three 60-minute compact discs.

2. *Living Language® Russian Coursebook.* This book is designed for use with the recorded lessons, but it may also be used alone as a reference. It contains the following sections:

   Basic Russian in 40 Lessons
   Summary of Russian Grammar
   Verb conjugations
   Letter writing

3. *Living Language® Russian Dictionary.* The Russian/English–English/Russian dictionary contains more than 15,000 entries. Phrases and idiomatic expressions illustrate many of the definitions. The most essential words are preceded by an *.

INSTRUCTIONS

1. Look at page 2. The words in **boldface** type are the ones you will hear on the recording.
2. Now read Lesson 1 all the way through. Note the points to listen for when you play the recording. The first word you will hear is **Алекса́ндр** (Alexander).
3. Start the recording, listen carefully, and say the words aloud in the pauses provided. Go through the lesson once, and don't worry if you can't pronounce everything correctly the first time around. Try it again and keep repeating the lesson until you are comfortable with it. The more often you listen and repeat, the longer you will remember the material.
4. Now go on to the next lesson. If you take a break between lessons, it's always good to review the previous lesson before starting on a new one.
5. In the manual, there are two kinds of quizzes. With matching quizzes, you must select the English translation of the Russian sentence. The other type requires you to fill in the blanks with the correct Russian word. If you make any mistakes, reread the section.
6. Even after you have finished the forty lessons and achieved a perfect score on the Final Quiz, keep practicing your Russian by listening to the recordings and speaking with Russian-speaking friends. For further study, try *Living Language® Ultimate Russian* and *Ultimate Russian Advanced.*

LIVING LANGUAGE®

RUSSIAN COURSEBOOK

REVISED & UPDATED

LESSON 1

A. The Letters and Sounds of The Russian Language

Listen, then repeat. Russian pronunciation will be easy once you learn the rules of pronunciation and reading, which hold true with very few exceptions. It is just as easy to say *ah* as it is to say *oh*, or to say *vast* as it is to say *fast*. But if you pronounce *f* where it should be *v*, or *oh* where it should be *ah*, or *eh* where it should be *ee*, you will speak with a foreign accent. Knowing these rules will help you to have a sound picture of the word you are learning and will help you to recognize it when it is spoken by the native; you want to understand as well as to speak!

Russian is *not* phonetic. You *don't* read it the way it is spelled. Many native Russians think they do; most of them are sure they do—they are wrong!

Learn word units. Always try to pronounce pronoun, preposition, and adjective together with the word they modify. Note that all words that have more than one syllable are marked with an accent mark. This is done only for the sake of the student. Accent marks will not be found in reading material outside of textbooks, but for the sake of proper pronunciation, it is necessary to memorize the stress in each word.

Russian punctuation varies little from that of English in the use of the semi-colon, colon, exclamation point, question mark, and period. However, the use of the comma is determined by concrete grammatical rules and generally does not, as in English, indicate a voice stop.

Remember that the Russian language is not phonetic. Each letter represents several sounds. It is important to keep this in mind at the beginning of your study and to acquire the proper speech habits at the very start.

The Russian language has twenty consonant letters representing thirty-five consonant sounds, since fifteen of these twenty letters can represent either soft or hard (palatalized or nonpalatalized) sounds. Three are hard only; two are soft only. There are ten vowels and one semi-vowel.

Softness, or palatalization, of consonants is indicated by the vowels: **е, ё, и, ю, я,** and **ь** (soft sign). When a consonant is followed by one of these vowels, the consonant is palatalized, i.e., it is soft. In palatalization, the articulation of a consonant in its alphabet (nonpalatalized) form is altered in a specific way: the place and manner of articulation remain the same, but the middle part of the speaker's tongue moves up to the palate to produce "palatalization." Palatalization in the Russian language has particular significance and should therefore be carefully studied, as the meaning of a word can be changed through palatalization. Listen carefully and try to imitate.

The alphabet is given in Lesson 3, but listening to the tape and looking at the spelling of the following names and words will help you to recognize the different sounds each letter can represent.

B. Names

Many Russian sounds are like English. Listen to and repeat the following Russian names and notice which sounds are similar and which are different:

Алекса́ндр	Alexander
Алексе́й	Alexis

Анто́н	Anthony
Бори́с	Boris
Валенти́н	Valentine
Варва́ра	Barbara
Ви́ктор	Victor
Влади́мир	Vladimir
Воло́дя	Volodya, dim. of Vladimir
Гео́ргий	George
Дави́д	David
Дими́трий	Dimitri
Евге́ний	Eugene
Екатери́на	Catherine
Еле́на	Helen
Елизаве́та	Elizabeth
Же́ня	Gene, dim. of Eugene or Eugenia
Заха́р	Zachary
Ива́н	John, Ivan
И́горь	Igor
Ири́на	Irene
Ка́тя	Kate, dim. of Catherine
Ко́ля	Kolya, dim. of Nicholas
Константи́н	Constantine
Леони́д	Leonid
Ли́за	Liza, dim. of Elizabeth
Любо́вь	Amy
Лю́ба	dim. of Amy
Людми́ла	Ludmilla
Макси́м	Maxim
Маргари́та	Margaret
Михаи́л	Michael
Наде́жда	Nadezhda
На́дя	Nadya, dim. of Nadezhda or Nadine
Ната́лия	Natalie

Ната́ша	Natasha, dim. of Natalie
Никола́й	Nicholas
О́льга	Olga
Па́вел	Paul
Пётр	Peter
Серге́й	Sergei
Фёдор	Theodore

NOTE

1. Each vowel is pronounced clearly, but the same letter does not always have the same sound. This is especially true of the letter *o*, which sometimes has the sound of *oh* but more often the sound of *ah*. The letter *e* sometimes has the sound of *eh* and sometimes the sound of *yeh*.
2. The accent mark (´) shows the syllable that is stressed. The stressed vowel is pronounced in its alphabet form, with more emphasis (slightly longer and louder).
3. Each word has only one stressed syllable.
4. Stress in the Russian language follows no rule. Any syllable can be stressed.
5. All syllables after the stressed syllable are pronounced with less emphasis.

Pay attention to the consonant and its palatalization.

C. Geographical Names

Австра́лия	Australia
А́зия	Asia
Аме́рика	America
Аргенти́на	Argentina
Арха́нгельск	Arkhangelsk
Байка́л	Baikal (Lake)
Баку́	Baku
Болга́рия	Bulgaria
Варша́ва	Warsaw

Вашингто́н	Washington
Великобрита́ния	Great Britain
Владивосто́к	Vladivostok
Во́лга	Volga
Гали́ция	Galicia
Герма́ния	Germany
Гру́зия	Georgia
Днепр	Dnieper
Дуна́й	Danube
Евро́па	Europe
Еги́пет	Egypt
И́ндия	India
Ита́лия	Italy
Иртыш	Irtisch (River)
Кавка́з	Caucasus
Калифо́рния	California
Ки́ев	Kiev
Константино́поль	Constantinople
Крым	Crimea
Македо́ния	Macedonia
Ме́ксика	Mexico
Москва́	Moscow
Нева́	Neva
Оде́сса	Odessa
Ока́	Oka
Псков	Pskov
Росси́я	Russia
Ряза́нь	Ryazan
Сама́ра	Samara
Севасто́поль	Sevastopol

LESSON 2

A. Cognates: Words Similar in Russian and English

Listen to these Russian words, which are general equivalents of English words. These words are descended from the same root and are called cognates. Note the character of Russian pronunciation as well as Russian intonation.

абсолюти́зм	absolutism
аванга́рд	avant-garde
авиа́ция	aviation
автобиогра́фия	autobiography
атмосфе́ра	atmosphere
бактериоло́гия	bacteriology
балла́да	ballad
баро́метр	barometer
батаре́я	battery
библиогра́фия	bibliography
вака́нсия	vacancy
вандали́зм	vandalism
витами́ны	vitamins
гара́нтия	guarantee
генера́тор	generator
геоло́гия	geology
гладиа́тор	gladiator
дарвини́зм	Darwinism
деклара́ция	declaration
демокра́тия	democracy
диа́гноз	diagnosis
диале́кт	dialect
дие́та	diet
дисципли́на	discipline
жонглёр	juggler

зигза́г	zigzag
игнори́ровать	ignore
иде́я	idea
имита́ция	imitation
индивидуали́зм	individualism
инспе́ктор	inspector
инстру́ктор	instructor
инструме́нт	instrument
калейдоско́п	kaleidoscope
карикату́ра	caricature
компози́тор	composer
коопера́ция	cooperation
корреспонде́нт	correspondent
кри́тика	criticism
лабири́нт	labyrinth
лаборато́рия	laboratory
либерали́зм	liberalism
литерату́ра	literature
марксизм	Marxism
медици́на	medicine
мето́дика	method
микроско́п	microscope
негати́в	negative
обсерваторія	observatory
о́пера	opera
опера́ция	operation
оппози́ция	opposition
оптими́ст	optimist
павильо́н	pavilion
панора́ма	panorama
паразит	parasite
перспекти́ва	perspective
пикни́к	picnic
пирами́да	pyramid
популя́рный	popular
привиле́гия	privilege

прогре́сс	progress
радиа́тор	radiator
раке́та	rocket
резервуа́р	reservoir
репута́ция	reputation
рефле́ктор	reflector
стати́стика	statistics
та́ктика	tactics
телеско́п	telescope
тео́рия	theory
терминоло́гия	terminology
увертю́ра	overture
университе́т	university
эволю́ция	evolution

B. Geographical Names II

Алжи́р	Algeria
А́встрия	Austria
А́нглия	England
Бе́льгия	Belgium
Брази́лия	Brazil
Гре́ция	Greece
Да́ния	Denmark
Изра́иль	Israel
Ирла́ндия	Ireland
Испа́ния	Spain
Кана́да	Canada
Кита́й	China
Коре́я	Korea
Люксембу́рг	Luxembourg
Маро́кко	Morocco
Нидерла́нды	Netherlands
Но́вая Зела́ндия	New Zealand
Норве́гия	Norway
Португа́лия	Portugal

Таила́нд	Thailand
Ту́рция	Turkey
Швейца́рия	Switzerland
Шве́ция	Sweden
Шотла́ндия	Scotland
Япо́ния	Japan

LESSON 3

A. Introduction to the Russian Alphabet

Russian uses the Cyrillic alphabet, which derives from the Greek, whereas English is written with the Latin alphabet. However, there are a few letters that are shared by both languages. Still other letters may be familiar to you from basic mathematics and the names of college fraternities and sororities. As you use this book, you will quickly become familiar with the different letters and sounds, and soon you'll be able to recognize them instantly.

B. The Alphabet

Russian	Letter Script		Name
Аа	*А*	*а*	ah
Бб	*Б*	*б*	beh
Вв	*В*	*в*	veh
Гг	*Г*	*г*	geh
Дд	*Д*	*д*	deh
Ее	*Е*	*е*	yeh
Ёё	*Ё*	*ё*	yoh
Жж	*Ж*	*ж*	zheh
Зз	*З*	*з*	zeh
Ии	*И*	*и*	ee
Йй	*Й*	*й*	y (i short)

Кк	*К*	*к*	kah
Лл	*Л*	*л*	ell
Мм	*М*	*м*	em
Нн	*Н*	*н*	en
Оо	*О*	*о*	oh
Пп	*П*	*п*	peh
Рр	*Р*	*р*	err
Сс	*С*	*с*	ess
Тт	*Т*	*т*	teh
Уу	*У*	*у*	ooh
Фф	*Ф*	*ф*	eff
Хх	*Х*	*х*	khah
Цц	*Ц*	*ц*	tseh
Чч	*Ч*	*ч*	cheh
Шш	*Ш*	*ш*	shah
Щщ	*Щ*	*щ*	shchah
Ыы	*Ы*	*ы*	yerih
Ьь	*Ь*	*ь*	soft sign
Ъъ	*Ъ*	*ъ*	hard sign
Ээ	*Э*	*э*	eh
Юю	*Ю*	*ю*	yoo
Яя	*Я*	*я*	yah

LESSON 4

A. Palatalized and Nonpalatalized Syllables

Here are all possible combinations of consonants followed by vowels. On the tape, each hard syllable is followed by the palatalized or soft syllable. Listen carefully and try to hear the difference. Imitate. Listen again. Try to hear the difference in your own pronunciation.

ба ва га да жа за ка ла ма на па ра са та фа ха ца ча ша ща

бя вя гя дя зя кя ля мя ня пя ря ся тя фя

бо во го до жо зо ко ло мо но по ро со то фо хо цо чо шо що

бё вё гё дё жё зё кё лё мё нё пё рё сё тё фё чё шё щё

бу ву гу ду жу зу ку лу му ну пу ру су ту фу ху цу чу шу щу

бю вю дю жю* зю кю лю мю ню пю рю сю тю фю хю

бэ вэ гэ дэ зэ кэ лэ мэ нэ пэ рэ сэ тэ фэ хэ цэ

бе ве ге де же зе ке ле ме не пе ре се те фе хе це че ше ще

* Pronounced soft (palatalized), as in жюри (jury), a word of foreign origin.

бы вы ды зы лы мы ны пы ры сы ты фы хы цы

би ви ги ди жи зи ки ли ми ни пи ри си ти фи хи ци чи ши щи

NOTE

Keep in mind the following points:

жо and жё	are pronounced alike.
цэ and це цы and ци шо and шё	the letters ж, ц, ш are always hard.
чо and чё що and щё	the letters ч and щ are always soft.

LESSON 5

A. Vowels

1. The letter А
   a. When stressed, it is pronounced like the English *ah*:

а́рмия	army
ла́мпа	lamp
ма́ло	little

   b. When unstressed, before a stressed syllable, it is pronounced *ah*, but shorter.

команди́р	commander
каде́т	cadet

   c. In most other positions it is given a neuter sound—i.e., like that of the letter *a* in *sofa*:

каранда́ш	pencil
магази́н	store
аванга́рд	avant-garde

2. The letter О
   a. When stressed, it is pronounced *oh,* as in *low*:

он	he
до́брый	pleasant

   b. When unstressed, it is either in first place before the stressed syllable or used initially and is pronounced *ah*:

Бори́с	Boris
она́	she
оно́	it
отвеча́ть	to answer

   c. In all other positions it is given a neuter sound—i.e., like the *a* in *sofa*:

хорошо́	well
пло́хо	badly
молоко́	milk

3. The letter У
   is pronounced both stressed and unstressed like the English *ooh*:

стул	chair
суп	soup
у́тро	morning
туда́	there (in that direction)
уро́к	lesson
узнава́ть	to find out
учи́тель	teacher

4. The letter **Ы**
   has no strict equivalent in English; however, it closely resembles the *i* sound in *sit*:

ты	you
мы	we
вы	you *(pl.)*
мы́ло	soap
малы́	small (predicative form)
столы́	tables
была́	she was

5. The letter **Э**
   is pronounced like the *eh* in *echo*:

э́то	this
э́ти	these
поэ́т	poet
эта́п	stage

NOTE

The function of the following vowels—**е, ё, и, ю, я**—which are preceded by a glide (the sound similar to the final sound in the English word *may*) is the palatalization of the preceding consonant, to which they lose the above-mentioned glide. However, when they follow a vowel or soft or hard signs, or when they appear initially, they are pronounced as in the alphabet—i.e., with an initial glide.

6. The letter **И**
   always palatalizes the preceding consonant and is pronounced like the *ee* in *beet* except after the letters **ж, ц, ш,** which are never palatalized; then **и** is pronounced like the Russian sound **ы:**

си́ла	strength
Ли́за	Liza

никогда́	never
иногда́	sometimes
ши́на[1]	tire
жить[1]	live

7. The letter **Й**
   a. It is never stressed. It is pronounced like the final sound in the English word *boy*:

мой	my
пойти́	to go
споко́йно	quietly

   b. It is very seldom used initially, except in some words of foreign origin:

Нью-Йорк	New York

8. The letter **Е**
   a. It always palatalizes the preceding consonant, except the letters **ж, ц, ш.** When stressed, it is pronounced like the *yeh* in *yet*:

нет	no, not
Ве́ра	Vera, faith
сесть	to sit down

   b. In unstressed positions it is pronounced like the soft *i* in *sit*:

всегда́	always
сестра́	sister
жена́	wife

[1] Here **и** is pronounced **ы** because **ж** and **ш** are never palatalized.

c. Initially, or after another vowel, it is pronounced with the glide stressed, like *yeh,* or unstressed, like *yeeh*:

ей	to her
её	her
пое́здка	trip

9. The letter **Ё**
always palatalizes the preceding consonant and is always stressed. It is pronounced like the *yo* in *yoke*:

мёд	honey
тётя	aunt
ёлка	fir tree
моё	my (*n*)
ещё	yet, still

10. The letter **Я**
a. It always palatalizes the preceding consonant. When stressed in the middle of the word, it is pronounced *yah;* when unstressed, it is pronounced either like the short *i* of *sit* or like the neutral *a* of *sofa* if it is the last letter of a word:

мя́со	meat
мая́к	lighthouse
тётя	aunt
де́сять	ten

b. When used initially, it retains its glide; when stressed, it is pronounced *yah;* when unstressed, *yih*:

я́блоко	apple
янва́рь	January
язы́к	language, tongue

11. The letter **Ю**
    a. It always palatalizes the preceding consonant. It is pronounced *ooh* in the body of the word:

Лю́ба	Lyuba
люблю́	I love
люби́ть	to love

    b. When used initially, it retains its glide and is pronounced *yooh*:

ю́бка	skirt
юбиле́й	jubilee

12. The letter **Ь**
    is called the "soft" sign; it palatalizes the preceding consonant, allowing the following vowel to retain its glide. It also indicates that the preceding consonant is soft when written at the end of a word:

пье́са	play
пья́ный	drunk
свинья́	pig

13. The letter **Ъ**
    is called the "hard" sign. It indicates that the preceding consonant remains hard and that the following vowel retains its glide:

объём	volume
объясня́ть	explain

LESSON 6

A. Consonants

Russian consonants, like those in every language, may be voiced or voiceless. The distinction between voiced and voiceless consonants is based on one aspect of otherwise identical articulation: in voiced consonants vocal cords are involved in articulation, while in voiceless consonants they are not. The pairs are:

б в г д ж з	(voiced)	b v g d zh z
п ф к т ш с	(voiceless)	p f k t sh s

When two consonants are pronounced together, both must be either voiced or voiceless. In Russian, the second one always remains as it is and the first one changes accordingly.

всё, все, вчера́	**в**=v, pronounced *f*
сде́лать, сдать	**с**=s, pronounced *z*

The preposition в (in) is very often pronounced *f*. В шко́ле (in school) is pronounced *fshkoh-leh*.

Russian consonants can also be soft or hard, i.e., palatalized or nonpalatalized, when followed by the letters е, ё, и, ю, я or ь; exceptions are the consonants ж, ш, ц, which are always hard.

This looks complicated, but it is much easier to learn this in the beginning and to begin speaking correctly than it is to try to correct erroneous pronunciation later on. Listen carefully and try to hear the above-mentioned differences.

Б

1. Pronounced like the *b* in *bread*:

брат	brother
бума́га	paper
бага́ж	baggage

2. Palatalized:

бе́лый	white
бино́кль	binoculars

3. Voiceless, like the *p* at the end of a word or before a voiceless consonant:

ю́бка	skirt
зуб	tooth
хлеб	bread

4. Voiceless palatalized:

дробь	buckshot
зыбь	ripple

В

1. Pronounced like the *v* in *very*:

ваш	your
вот	here
вода́	water

2. Palatalized:

ве́ра	faith
конве́рт	envelope
весь	all

3. Voiceless, like the *f* at the end of a word or before a voiceless consonant:

Ки́ев	Kiev
в шко́ле	in school
вчера́	yesterday
кров	shelter

4. Voiceless palatalized:

кровь	blood

Г

1. Pronounced like the *g* in *good*:

газе́та	newspaper
где	where
гармо́ния	harmony

2. Palatalized:

гита́ра	guitar
геоме́трия	geometry

3. Like the Russian **х** before **к:**

легко́	lightly, easily
мя́гко	softly

4. Like the *v* in the genitive ending, masculine and neuter:

его́	his
ничего́	nothing
сего́дня	today

5. Voiceless, like the *k* at the end of a word:

рог	horn
четве́рг	Thursday

Д

1. Pronounced like the *d* in *door*:

дом	house
родно́й	kindred

2. Palatalized:

де́рево	wood
оди́н	one

3. Voiceless, like the *t* at the end of a word or before a voiceless consonant:

обе́д	dinner
подко́ва	horseshoe
по́дпись	signature

4. Voiceless palatalized:

грудь	breast

Ж

1. Pronounced like the *s* in *measure*: always hard:

жар	heat
жена́	wife
жить	to live
пожа́р	fire

2. Voiceless, like the *sh* at the end of a word or before a voiceless consonant:

ло́жка	spoon
муж	husband

З

1. Pronounced like the *z* in *zebra*:

зда́ние	building
знать	to know

2. Palatalized:

зелёный	green
зима́	winter

3. Voiceless, like the *s* at the end of a word or before a voiceless consonant:

ползти́	crawl
воз	cart

К

1. Pronounced like the *k* in *kept*:

кни́га	book
класс	class
каранда́ш	pencil

2. Palatalized:

ке́пка	cap
кероси́н	kerosene
Ки́ев	Kiev
кино́	movie

3. Voiced, like the *g* in *good,* before a voiced consonant:

вокза́л	railroad station
экза́мен	examination
к бра́ту	to the brother

Л

1. Pronounced like the *l* in *look*:

ло́жка	spoon
ла́мпа	lamp
мел	chalk

2. Palatalized:

любо́вь	love
лёгкий	light
мель	shoal
боль	pain

LESSON 7

A. Consonants II

М

1. Pronounced like the *m* in *man*:

ма́ма	mama
магни́т	magnet
дом	house
паро́м	ferry

2. Palatalized:

мя́со	meat
ми́на	mine

Н

1. Pronounced like the *n* in *noon*:

нос	nose
нож	knife
балко́н	balcony

2. Palatalized:

не́бо	sky
неде́ля	week
ня́ня	nurse
ко́нь	horse

П

1. Palatalized:

пе́рвый	first
письмо́	letter
цепь	chain

Р

1. Pronounced like the *r* in *root*:

ру́сский	Russian
пара́д	parade
пода́рок	gift
рука́	hand

2. Palatalized:

рис	rice
поря́док	order
дверь	door

С

1. Pronounced like the *s* in *see*:

сон	dream
суп	soup
свет	light
мя́со	meat
ма́сло	butter

2. Palatalized:

се́вер	north
село́	village
весь	all

3. Voiced, like the *z* before a voiced consonant:

сде́лать	to do
сгоре́ть	to burn down

Т

1. Pronounced like the *t* in *table*:

таба́к	tobacco
тот	that
стол	table
тогда́	then

2. Palatalized:

тень	shade
стена́	wall

3. Voiced like the *d* before a voiced consonant:

отда́ть	to give away
отгада́ть	to guess

Ф

1. Pronounced like the *f* in *friend*:

фа́брика	factory
Фра́нция	France
фарфо́р	porcelain

2. Palatalized:

афи́ша	poster

3. Voiced, like the *v* before a voiced consonant:

афга́нец	Afghan

Х

1. Pronounced like the *kh* in *loch*:

ти́хо	quietly
хорошо́	well
те́хника	technique
блоха́	flea

2. Palatalized

хи́на	quinine
хи́мия	chemistry

Ц

Pronounced like the *ts* in *gets;* always hard:

цвето́к	flower
цепь	chain
цирк	circus
паци́ент	patient (*n.*)
пе́рец	pepper

Ч

1. Pronounced like the *ch* in *church;* always soft:

чай	tea
час	hour
ча́сто	often
чемода́н	suitcase

2. Sometimes pronounced like the *sh* in *shall*:

что	what
коне́чно	of course

Ш

Pronounced like the *sh* in *shall;* always hard:

шаг за ша́гом	step after step
ша́хматы	chess
ши́на	tire
шёлк	silk
шерсть	wool
ты говори́шь	you speak *(sing.)*

Щ

Pronounced like the *shch* in the word combination *fresh cheese;* always soft:

щека́	cheek
щётка	brush
по́мощь	help
посеще́ние	visit

This completes the rules for pronunciation and reading. Read these rules over and over again. Listen to the tapes over and over again. You have learned them not when you have read and understood the rules, but when you can remember and repeat the sounds and words correctly without looking at the book. Master these, and you will speak Russian well.

FIVE FUNDAMENTAL RULES

1. Remember which syllable is stressed.
2. Remember that unstressed о is pronounced *ah* in prestressed position.
3. Remember that when two consonants are next to each other, the first changes according to the second.
4. Remember that unstressed е is pronounced *ih*.
5. Remember that the letters е, ё, и, ю, я, and ь palatalize the preceding consonant unless it has no palatalized counterpart.

LESSON 8

A. Masculine, Feminine, Neuter, Plural

All Russian nouns, pronouns, adjectives, and ordinal numbers, as well as some cardinal numbers and even several verb forms, have gender: masculine, feminine, or neuter. In the plural there is only one form for all genders.

1. Most nouns, pronouns, and past tense forms of verbs end in:

MASCULINE	FEMININE	NEUTER	PLURAL
hard consonant	а, я	о, е	а, ы, и

2. Most adjectives, ordinal numbers, and participles end in:

MASCULINE	FEMININE	NEUTER	PLURAL
ой, ый, ий	ая, яя	ое, ее	ые, ие
он	**она́**	**оно́**	**они́**
he	she	it	they
мой	**моя́**	**моё**	**мои́**
my	my	my	my
мой брат	**моя́ сестра́**	**моё окно́**	**мои́ де́ти**
my brother	my sister	my window	my children
твой	**твоя́**	**твоё**	**твои́**
your *(sing., fam.)*	your	your	your
твой	**твоя́**	**твоё**	**твои́**
каранда́ш	**кни́га**	**пальто́**	**де́ньги**
your pencil	your book	your coat	your money
наш дом	**на́ша**	**на́ше**	**на́ши**
	кварти́ра	**село́**	**кни́ги**
our house	our apartment	our village	our books
ваш	**ва́ша**	**ва́ше**	**ва́ши**
your *(pl., polite)*	your	your	your
ваш стул	**ва́ша ла́мпа**	**ва́ше по́ле**	**ва́ши руба́шки**
your chair	your lamp	your field	your shirts
э́тот	**э́та**	**э́то**	**э́ти**
this	this	this	these
бе́лый	**бе́лая**	**бе́лое**	**бе́лые**
white	white	white	white
Э́тот стол бе́лый.	**Э́та стена́ бе́лая.**	**Э́то пла́тье бе́лое.**	**Э́ти сте́ны бе́лые.**
This table is white.	This wall is white.	This dress is white.	These walls are white.
большо́й	**больша́я**	**большо́е**	**больши́е**
large	large	large	large
его́	**её**	**его́**	**их**
his	her	its	their
его́ оте́ц	**её оте́ц**		**их оте́ц**
his father	her father		their father
чей оте́ц	**чья мать**	**чьё окно́**	**чьи кни́ги**
whose father	whose mother	whose window	whose books
свой	**своя́**	**своё**	**свои́**
one's own	one's own	one's own	one's own

кра́сный	**кра́сная**	**кра́сное**	**кра́сные**
red	red	red	red
чёрный	**чёрная**	**чёрное**	**чёрные**
black	black	black	black
си́ний	**си́няя**	**си́нее**	**си́ние**
blue	blue	blue	blue
оди́н	**одна́**	**одно́**	**оди́н**
one	one	one	alone, only
два	**две**	**два**	
two	two	two	
пе́рвый	**пе́рвая**	**пе́рвое**	**пе́рвые**
first	first	first	first
второ́й	**втора́я**	**второ́е**	**вторы́е**
second	second	second	second
тре́тий	**тре́тья**	**тре́тье**	**тре́тьи**
third	third	third	third

NOTE

Pronouns, adjectives, and ordinal numbers always agree in gender with the nouns they modify.

QUIZ 1

Match the Russian words with the correct English translations.

1. оди́н	a. this (m.)
2. кра́сная	b. my children
3. де́ньги	c. This wall is white.
4. он	d. our books
5. ва́ша ла́мпа	e. her
6. Э́та стена́ бе́лая.	f. he
7. э́тот	g. first (f.)
8. на́ши кни́ги	h. red (f.)
9. мои́ де́ти	i. children
10. мой брат	j. one (m.)
11. её	k. these
12. де́ти	l. money
13. пе́рвая	m. your field
14. ва́ше по́ле	n. your lamp
15. э́ти	o. my sister
16. моя́ сестра́	p. my brother

ANSWERS

1—j; 2—h; 3—l; 4—f; 5—n; 6—c; 7—a; 8—d; 9—b; 10—p; 11—e; 12—i; 13—g; 14—m; 15—k; 16—o.

LESSON 9

A. Characteristics of the Cases

With few exceptions, all nouns, pronouns, and adjectives decline. Each declension has six cases used to answer the following question words in their respective case forms (some preceded by the appropriate prepositions):

CASE	QUESTIONS
Nominative (subject):	**Кто? Что?** Who? What?
Genitive (possession, negation):	**Кого́? Чего́?** Whom? What? **От кого́? От чего́?** From whom? From what? **У кого́? У чего́?** At/by whom? At/by what? **Без кого́? Без чего́?** Without whom? Without what?
Dative (indirect object):	**Кому́? Чему́?** To whom? To what? **К кому́? К чему́?** Toward whom? Toward what?
Accusative (direct object):	**Кого́? Что?** Whom? What? **Куда́?** Where (direction toward)?

Instrumental (object as an instrument, manner of action):	**Кем? Чем?** By whom? By what? **С кем? С чем?** With whom? With what?
Prepositional or Locative (location, also with certain prepositions):	**О ком? О чём?** About whom? About what? **В ком? В чём?** In whom? In what? **Где?** Where?

1. The nominative case supplies the subject of the sentence.

2. The genitive is the case of possession and is also used with many prepositions, the most common of which are без (without), для (for), до (up to), из (out of), о́коло (near by, about), от (from), по́сле (after), and у (at or by).

3. The dative case is used in the meaning of "to whom." Prepositions governing the dative case are к (to) and по (along).

4. The accusative is the direct-object case. Prepositions used with this case include в (to, into), за (behind), and на (to, into, on) in the sense of direction.

5. The instrumental case indicates the manner of action or the instrument with which the action is performed. Prepositions governing the instrumental case include ме́жду (between), пе́ред (in front of), and с (with).

6. The prepositional or locative case indicates location, but it is also used when speaking about something or someone. The prepositions most frequently used with this case are в (in), на (on), о (about), and при (in the presence of).

B. Word Study

звони́ть-позвони́ть*	to call (on the phone)
почему́	why
вме́сте	together
потому́ что	because
говори́ть-сказа́ть	to say
уже́	already
непра́вильно	incorrectly
ка́ждый	each, every
зада́ча	problem, task

LESSON 10

A. Кто (Who?) and Никто́/Не́кто (No One/Someone)

NOTE

When used with prepositions, the negative expressions никто́/не́кто split into three words: the negative particle ни/не, the preposition, and the declined form of кто. (Никто́ is used only with negated verbs, не́кто only with non-negated verbs, primarily in impersonal sentences). This will be clear after you study these phrases.

* This pair of verbs represents an aspectual pair of verbs, a characteristic of Russian which will be discussed later.

NOMINATIVE:

Кто он?	Who is he?
Кто она́?	Who is she?
Кто они́?	Who are they?
Кто э́то сде́лал?	Who did this?
Кто сказа́л э́то?	Who said this?

NEGATIVE:

Никто́ не сде́лал.	No one did this.
Никто́ не сказа́л.	No one said it.

GENITIVE:

Кого́ нет до́ма?	Who is not at home?
у кого́ он живёт?	At whose place (by whom) does he live?
Для кого́ э́то?	For whom is that?

NEGATIVE:

Никого́ нет до́ма.	No one is at home.
Э́то ни для кого́.	This is for no one.
Не у кого́ жить.	There is no one to live with (at).

DATIVE:

Кому́ вы э́то сказа́ли?	To whom did you say that?
Кому́ вы да́ли мою́ кни́гу?	To whom did you give my book?
К кому́ вы идёте?	To whom (whose home) are you going?
Кому́ здесь хо́лодно?	Who is cold here? (To whom is it cold?)

NEGATIVE:

Не говори́те никому́.	Don't tell anyone.
Не́кому написа́ть.	There's no one to write to.

ACCUSATIVE:

Кого́ вы зна́ете здесь?	Whom do you know here?

На кого́ она́ похо́жа?	Whom does she look like?

NEGATIVE:

Я здесь никого́ не зна́ю.	I don't know anyone here.
Не на кого́ положи́ться.	Nobody to rely on.

INSTRUMENTAL:

С кем вы бы́ли в теа́тре вчера́?	With whom were you at the theater yesterday?
Кем вы хоти́те быть?	What do you want to be?

NEGATIVE:

Я ни с кем не был в теа́тре.	I was with no one at the theater.
Не с кем поговори́ть.	Nobody to talk to.

LOCATIVE/PREPOSITIONAL:

О ком вы говори́те?	Whom are you talking about?
На ком он жена́т?	To whom is he married?

NEGATIVE:

Мы ни о ком не говори́м.	We are not talking about anyone.
Он ни на ком не жена́т.	He is not married to anyone.

QUIZ 2

Fill in the blanks with the proper form of **кто.**

1. _____ сказа́л э́то?	Who said it?
2. _____ нет до́ма?	Who isn't at home?
3. _____ здесь хо́лодно?	Who is cold here?

4. _____ вы да́ли мою́ кни́гу?	To whom did you give my book?
5. _____ вы хоти́те быть?	What do you want to be?
6. На _____ он жена́т?	To whom is he married?
7. Не с _____ говори́ть.	No one to talk with.
8. _____ вы зна́ете здесь?	Whom do you know here?
9. Я _____ здесь не зна́ю.	I don't know anyone here.
10. О _____ вы говори́те?	Whom are you talking about?

ANSWERS

1. Кто 2. Кого́ 3. Кому́ 4. Кому́ 5. Кем 6. ком 7. кем 8. Кого́ 9. никого́ 10. ком.

B. Что? (What?) and Ничего́/Не́чего (Nothing)

NOTE

As with никто́/не́кто, when used with prepositions, the negative expressions ничего́/не́чего split into three words: the particle ни/не, the preposition, and the declined form of что (чего́ in ничего́/не́чего is the genitive form of что).

NOMINATIVE:

Что э́то?	What is it?
Что там?	What's there?
Я не зна́ю, что э́то.	I don't know what it is.
Что э́то тако́е?	What is this?
Что э́то за зда́ние?	What kind of a building is this?
Что но́вого?	What's new?
Что зна́чит э́то сло́во?	What does this word mean?
Что он сказа́л?	What did he say?

SET EXPRESSION:

Ни за что на све́те!	Not for anything in the world!

GENITIVE:

Для чего́ э́то?	What's this for?
Чего́ то́лько нет в э́том магази́не!	What they don't have in this store!
От чего́ у меня́ боли́т голова́?	Why [what from] does my head ache?

NEGATIVE:

Он ничего́ не сказа́л.	He didn't say anything.
В э́том магази́не ничего́ нет.	There is nothing in this store.
Не́чего беспоко́иться.	Don't you worry! (rude).

SET EXPRESSION:

Посмотри́те, до чего́ э́то дошло́.	Look what it has come to.
Чего́ он то́лько не ви́дел!	What hasn't he seen!

DATIVE:

Чему́ вы удивля́етесь?	What are you surprised at?
К чему́ всё э́то?	What's all this for?

NEGATIVE:

Э́то ни к чему́.	This is unnecessary [for nothing].
Не́чему удивля́ться.	Nothing to be surprised at.

SET EXPRESSION:

Чему́ быть—того́ не минова́ть.	What's to be, will be.

ACCUSATIVE:

Что вы хоти́те посмотре́ть?	What would you like to see?

NEGATIVE:

Не на что жить.	Nothing to live on.

INSTRUMENTAL:

Чем вы пи́шете?	What are you writing with?
Заче́м вы пришли́?	Why [what for] did you come?

NEGATIVE:

Она́ меня́ ниче́м не мо́жет удиви́ть.	She cannot surprise me with anything.

LOCATIVE/PREPOSITIONAL:

О чём вы говори́те?	What are you talking about?
При чём тут я?	What do I have to do with it?

NEGATIVE:

Я ни о чём не говорю́.	I am not talking about anything.
Не о чём сейча́с писа́ть.	There is nothing to write about now.

SET EXPRESSION:

В чём де́ло?	What's the matter?

C. Declensions of Nouns, Adjectives, and Pronouns

Here are the basic forms of declensions of nouns, adjectives, and pronouns.

Do not try to learn these forms. It is better to remember sentences as you continue with the tapes. As you learn sentences, you can refer to these tables to find out to which group the new words belong.

Grammar is a description of a language, not a set of rules by which a language should abide. Grammar describes many different groups in the language and many exceptions to these groups. The more groups and the more exceptions there are, the richer the language.

1. Nouns

	Masculine Singular			
	Hard		Soft	
	Animate	Inanimate	Animate	Inanimate
	student	question	inhabitant	shed
Nom.	студе́нт	вопро́с	жи́тель	сара́-й
Gen.	студе́нт-а	вопро́с-а	жи́тел-я	сара́-я
Dat.	студе́нт-у	вопро́с-у	жи́тел-ю	сара́-ю
Acc.	студе́нт-а	вопро́с	жи́тел-я	сара́-й
Inst.	студе́нт-ом	вопро́с-ом	жи́тел-ем	сара́-ем
Prep.	о студе́нт-е	о вопро́с-е	о жи́тел-е	о сара́-е

	Masculine Plural			
Nom.	студе́нт-ы	вопро́с-ы	жи́тел-и	сара́-и
Gen.	студе́нт-ов	вопро́с-ов	жи́тел-ей	сара́-ев
Dat.	студе́нт-ам	вопро́с-ам	жи́тел-ям	сара́-ям
Acc.	студе́нт-ов	вопро́с-ы	жи́тел-ей	сара́-и
Inst.	студе́нт-ами	вопро́с-ами	жи́тел-ями	сара́-ями
Prep.	о студе́нт-ах	о вопро́с-ах	о жи́тел-ях	о сара́-ях

NOTE

The accusative case of animate masculine nouns is the same as the genitive, while the accusative of inanimate masculine nouns is the same as the nominative.

	Feminine Singular		
	Hard	Soft	
	room	earth	family
Nom.	ко́мната	земля́	семья́
Gen.	ко́мнат-ы	земл-и́	семь-и́
Dat.	ко́мнат-е	земл-е́	семь-е́
Acc.	ко́мнат-у	зе́мл-ю	семь-ю́
Inst.	ко́мнат-ой(ою)	земл-ёй	семь-ёй
Prep.	о ко́мнат-е	о земл-е́	о семь-е́

	Feminine Plural		
Nom.	ко́мнат-ы	зе́мл-и	се́мь-и
Gen.	ко́мнат	земе́л-ь	сем-е́й
Dat.	ко́мнат-ам	зе́мл-ям	се́мь-ям
Acc.	ко́мнат-ы	зе́мл-и	се́мь-и
Inst.	ко́мнат-ами	зе́мл-ями	се́мь-ями
Prep.	о ко́мнат-ах	о зе́мл-ях	о се́мь-ях

	Neuter Singular		
	Hard	Soft	
	window	sea	wish
Nom.	окно́	мо́ре	жела́ние
Gen.	окн-а́	мо́р-я	жела́н-ия
Dat.	окн-у́	мо́р-ю	жела́н-ию
Acc.	окн-о́	мо́р-е	жела́н-ие
Inst.	окн-о́м	мо́р-ем	жела́н-ием
Prep.	об[1] окн-е́	о мо́р-е	о жела́н-ии

	Neuter Plural		
Nom.	о́кн-а	мор-я́	жела́н-ия
Gen.	о́к-он	мор-е́й	жела́н-ий
Dat.	о́кн-ам	мор-я́м	жела́н-иям
Acc.	о́кн-а	мор-я́	жела́н-ия
Inst.	о́кн-ами	мор-я́ми	жела́н-иями
Prep.	об[1] о́кн-ах	о мор-я́х	о жела́н-иях

[1] **б** is added to the preposition here for the sake of euphony.

2. Some Irregular Declensions

	Singular			
	Masc.	Fem.	Neut.	
	ROAD	MOTHER	NAME	CHILD
Nom.	путь	мать	и́мя	дитя́
Gen.	пут-и́	ма́т-ери	и́м-ени	дит-я́ти[1]
Dat.	пут-и́	ма́т-ери	и́м-ени	дит-я́ти[1]
Acc.	путь	мать	и́мя	дитя́
Inst.	пут-ём	ма́т-ерью	и́м-енем	дит-я́тей[1]
Prep.	о пут-и́	о ма́т-ери	об и́м-ени	о дит-я́ти[1]

	Plural			
Nom	пут-и́	ма́т-ери	име-на́	де́т-и
Gen.	пут-е́й	мат-ере́й	им-ён	дет-е́й
Dat.	пут-я́м	мат-еря́м	им-ена́м	де́т-ям
Acc.	пут-и́	мат-ере́й[2]	им-ена́	дет-е́й[2]
Inst.	пут-я́ми	мат-еря́ми	им-ена́ми	дет-ьми́
Prep.	о пут-я́х	о мат-еря́х	об им-ена́х	о де́т-ях

3. Adjectives

	Singular		
	New		
	MASC.	FEM.	NEUT.
	ый	ая	ое
Nom.	но́вый	но́вая	но́вое
Gen.	но́в-ого	но́в-ой	но́в-ого
Dat.	но́в-ому	но́в-ой	но́в-ому
Acc.	same as nom. or gen.[3]	но́в-ую	но́в-ое
Inst.	но́в-ым	но́в-ой(ою)	но́в-ым
Prep.	о но́в-ом	о но́в-ой	о но́в-ом

[1] Old form seldom used.
[2] The accusative plural of animate neuter nouns and most feminine nouns is the same as the genitive plural.
[3] See Note, p. 40.

	DEAR		
	ой	ая	ое
Nom.	дорого́й	дорога́я	дорого́е
Gen.	дорог-о́го	дорог-о́й	дорог-о́го
Dat.	дорог-о́му	дорог-о́й	дорог-о́му
Acc.	same as nom. or gen.	дорог-у́ю	дорог-о́е
Inst.	дорог-и́м	дорог-о́й(-о́ю)	дорог-и́м
Prep.	о дорог-о́м	о дорог-о́й	о дорог-о́м

	PLURAL	
	ALL GENDERS	
Nom.	но́в-ые	дорог-и́е
Gen.	но́в-ых	дорог-и́х
Dat.	но́в-ым	дорог-и́м
Acc.	same as nom. or gen.	same as nom. or gen.
Inst.	но́в-ыми	дорог-и́ми
Prep.	о но́в-ых	о дорог-и́х

	BLUE			
	SINGULAR			PLURAL
	MASC.	FEM.	NEUT.	ALL GENDERS
	ий	яя	ее	ие
Nom.	си́н-ий	си́н-яя	си́н-ее	си́н-ие
Gen.	си́н-его	си́н-ей	си́н-его	си́н-их
Dat.	си́н-ему	си́н-ей	си́н-ему	си́н-им
Acc.	same as nom. or gen.	си́н-юю	си́н-ее	same as nom. or gen.
Inst.	си́н-им	си́н-ей(-ею)	си́н-им	си́н-ими
Prep.	о си́н-ем	о си́н-ей	о си́н-ем	о си́н-их

4. Pronouns

	Singular				
	1st Person	2nd Person	3rd Person		
			Masc.	Neut.	Fem.
Nom.	я	ты	он	оно́	она́
Gen.	меня́	тебя́	его́	его́	её
Dat.	мне	тебе́	ему́	ему́	ей
Acc.	меня́	тебя́	его́	его́	её
Instr.	мной(-о́ю)	тобо́й(-о́ю)	им	им	ей, е́ю
Prep.	обо мне́	о тебе́	о нём	о нём	о ней

	Plural		
	1st Person	2nd Person	3rd Person
Nom.	мы	вы	они́
Gen.	нас	вас	их
Dat.	нам	вам	им
Acc.	нас	вас	их
Instr.	на́ми	ва́ми	и́ми
Prep.	о нас	о вас	о них

Reflexive Pronoun
Sing. or Plural
—
себя́
себе́
себя́
собо́й(-о́ю)
о себе́

	My			
	Singular			Plural
	Masc.	Fem.	Neuter	All genders
Nom.	мой	моя́	моё	мои́
Gen.	моего́	мое́й	моего́	мои́х
Dat.	моему́	мое́й	моему́	мои́м
Acc.	same as nom. or gen.	мою́	моё	same as nom. or gen.
Inst.	мои́м	мое́й(-е́ю)	мои́м	мои́ми
Prep.	о моём	о мое́й	о моём	о мои́х

NOTE

Твой (your, *sing.*), свой (one's own, their own) are declined in the same way as мой.

In expressing the possessive in the third person, the genitive case of the pronouns он, она́, оно́, они́—его́ (his), её (hers), его́ (its), их (theirs)—is used. These pronouns always agree with the gender and number of the possessor.

Их дом хоро́ший.	Their house is nice.
Я ви́дела их дочь.	I saw their daughter.
Он взял её кни́ги.	He took her books.
Его́ кни́га бо́лее интере́сная.	His book is more interesting.

	OUR			
	SINGULAR			PLURAL
	MASC.	FEM.	NEUTER	ALL GENDERS
Nom.	наш	на́ша	на́ше	на́ши
Gen.	на́ш-его	на́ш-ей	на́ш-его	на́ш-их
Dat.	на́ш-ему	на́ш-ей	на́ш-ему	на́ш-им
Acc.	same as nom. or gen.	на́ш-у	на́ше	same as nom. or gen.
Inst.	на́ш-им	на́ш-ей(-ею)	на́ш-им	на́ш-ими
Prep.	о на́ш-ем	о на́ш-ей	о на́ш-ем	о на́ш-их

NOTE

Ваш (your, *pl. or polite*) is declined in the same way.

	ALL			
	SINGULAR			PLURAL
	MASC.	FEM.	NEUTER	ALL GENDERS
Nom.	весь	вся	всё	все
Gen.	вс-его́	вс-ей	вс-его́	вс-ех
Dat.	вс-ему́	вс-ей	вс-ему́	вс-ем
Acc.	same as nom. or gen.	вс-ю	всё	same as nom. or gen.
Inst.	вс-ем	вс-ей(-ею)	вс-ем	вс-е́ми
Prep.	обо вс-ём	обо вс-ей	обо вс-ём	обо вс-ех

	Singular			Plural
	this			these
	Masc.	Fem.	Neuter	All genders
Nom.	э́тот	э́та	э́то	э́ти
Gen.	э́т-ого	э́т-ой	э́т-ого	э́т-их
Dat.	э́т-ому	э́т-ой	э́т-ому	э́т-им
Acc.	same as nom. or gen.	э́т-у	э́то	same as nom. or gen.
Inst.	э́т-им	э́т-ой	э́т-им	э́т-ими
Prep.	об э́т-ом	об э́т-ой	об э́т-ом	об э́т-их

	Singular			Plural
	that			those
	Masc.	Fem.	Neuter	All genders
Nom.	тот	та	то	те
Gen.	т-ого́	т-ой	т-ого́	т-ех
Dat.	т-ому́	т-ой	т-ому́	т-ем
Acc.	same as nom. or gen.	т-у	т-о	same as nom. or gen.
Inst.	т-ем	т-ой	т-ем	т-е́ми
Prep.	о т-ом	о т-ой	о т-ом	о т-ех

	Singular			Plural
	oneself			themselves
	Masc.	Fem.	Neuter	All genders
Nom.	сам	сама́	само́	са́ми
Gen.	сам-ого́	сам-о́й	сам-ого́	сам-и́х
Dat.	сам-ому́	сам-о́й	сам-ому́	сам-и́м
Acc.	same as nom. or gen.	сам-у́	сам-о́	same as nom. or gen.
Inst.	сам-и́м	сам-о́й	сам-и́м	сам-и́ми
Prep.	о сам-о́м	о сам-о́й	о сам-о́м	о сам-и́х

QUIZ 3

Fill in the blanks with the proper form of что.

1. Я не зна́ю, _____ э́то. I don't know what it is.
2. _____ но́вого? What's new?

3. _____ вы пи́шете? What are you writing?
4. Для _____ э́то? What's this for?
5. К _____ всё э́то? What's all this for?
6. _____ быть–того́ не минова́ть. What's to be, will be.
7. _____ вы удивля́етесь? What are you surprised at?
8. О _____ вы говори́те? What are you talking about?
9. В _____ де́ло? What's the matter?
10. _____ вы пи́шете? What are you writing with?

ANSWERS

1. что 2. Что 3. Что 4. чего́ 5. чему́ 6. Чему́ 7. Чему́ 8. чём 9. чём 10. Чем.

LESSON 11

A. Numbers 1–10

оди́н	one
два	two
три	three
четы́ре	four
пять	five
шесть	six
семь	seven
во́семь	eight
де́вять	nine
де́сять	ten

B. Days and Months[1]

понеде́льник	Monday
вто́рник	Tuesday
среда́	Wednesday

[1] Neither the names of the days nor of the months are capitalized unless they are found at the beginning of a sentence.

четве́рг	Thursday
пя́тница	Friday
суббо́та	Saturday
воскресе́нье	Sunday
янва́рь	January
февра́ль	February
март	March
апре́ль	April
май	May
ию́нь	June
ию́ль	July
а́вгуст	August
сентя́брь	September
октя́брь	October
ноя́брь	November
дека́брь	December

C. Seasons and Directions

весна́	spring
весно́й	in the spring
ле́то	summer
ле́том	in the summer
о́сень	autumn
о́сенью	in the autumn
зима́	winter
зимо́й	in the winter
се́вер	north
юг	south
восто́к	east
за́пад	west

D. Word Study

ма́льчик	boy
де́вочка	girl

пока́зывать-показа́ть	to show
свобо́дный	free
повторя́ть-повтори́ть	to repeat
иногда́	sometimes
ме́дленно	slowly

LESSON 12

A. Greetings

у́тро	morning
у́тром	in the morning
день	day
днём	during the day (afternoon)
ве́чер	evening
ве́чером	in the evening
ночь	night
но́чью	during the night
сего́дня	today
вчера́	yesterday
за́втра	tomorrow
до́брое	good
у́тро	morning
До́брое у́тро.	Good morning.
до́брый	good
день	day/afternoon
До́брый день.	Good day. Good afternoon.
ве́чер	evening
До́брый ве́чер.	Good evening.
как	how
дела́	things
Как дела́?	How are things?
как	how
вы	you
себя́	yourself

чу́вствуете	feel
Как вы себя́ чу́вствуете?	How are you feeling?
спаси́бо	thank you
хорошо́	well
Спаси́бо, хорошо́.	Well, thank you.
ничего́	nothing
Спаси́бо, ничего́.	Thank you, not bad.
нельзя́	impossible [one may not]
лу́чше	better
Как нельзя́ лу́чше.	Couldn't be any better.
А вы?	And you?
То́же хорошо́, спаси́бо.	Also well, thank you.
Прекра́сно.	Excellent.
Что но́вого?	What's new?
Всё по-ста́рому.	Everything's the same [all as of old].

B. Last Month, Last Year, etc.

послеза́втра	day after tomorrow
че́рез два дня	in two days
че́рез пять дней	in five days
че́рез ме́сяц	in a month
на про́шлой неде́ле	last week
две неде́ли тому́ наза́д	two weeks ago
в про́шлом ме́сяце	last month
в про́шлом году́	last year
позавчера́	day before yesterday
вчера́ ве́чером	yesterday evening
за́втра у́тром	tomorrow morning
три дня тому́ наза́д	three days ago
ме́сяц тому́ наза́д	a month ago

QUIZ 4

Match the Russian terms with their English translations.

1. среда́	a. in the evening
2. семь	b. north
3. март	c. tomorrow
4. сего́дня	d. Thank you.
5. Как дела́?	e. Well, thank you.
6. ве́чером	f. Good evening.
7. день	g. Tuesday
8. се́вер	h. Wednesday
9. вто́рник	i. Monday
10. октя́брь	j. winter
11. Спаси́бо.	k. seven
12. восто́к	l. in the morning
13. ле́то	m. impossible [one may not]
14. До́брый ве́чер.	n. today
15. нельзя́	o. summer
16. за́втра	p. March
17. у́тром	q. east
18. понеде́льник	r. day
19. зима́	s. October
20. Спаси́бо, хорошо́	t. How are you?

ANSWERS

1—h; 2—k; 3—p; 4—n; 5—t; 6—a; 7—r; 8—b; 9—g; 10—s; 11—d; 12—q; 13—o; 14—f; 15—m; 16—c; 17—l; 18—i; 19—j; 20—e.

LESSON 13

A. Common Verb Forms

Russian verbs have two conjugations. Infinitives of most verbs belonging to the first conjugation end with -ать or -ять. Infinitives of verbs belonging to the second conjugation end with -еть or -ить. Although this is true of a great number of Russian verbs, there are many exceptions, which will be explained as they appear in the text.

Following are typical conjugations in the present tense:

First Conjugation

читáть	TO READ
я читáю	I read
ты читáешь	you read
он читáет	he reads
мы читáем	we read
вы читáете	you read
онú читáют	they read

знать	TO KNOW
я знáю	I know
ты знáешь	you know
он знáет	he knows
мы знáем	we know
вы знáете	you know
онú знáют	they know

понимáть	TO UNDERSTAND
я понимáю	I understand
ты понимáешь	you understand
он понимáет	he understands
мы понимáем	we understand
вы понимáете	you understand
онú понимáют	they understand

ДУ́МАТЬ	TO THINK
я ду́маю	I think
ты ду́маешь	you think
он ду́мает	he thinks
мы ду́маем	we think
вы ду́маете	you think
они́ ду́мают	they think

писа́ть[1]	TO WRITE
я пишу́	I write
ты пи́шешь	you write
он пи́шет	he writes
мы пи́шем	we write
вы пи́шете	you write
они́ пи́шут	they write

Verbs ending with -нуть in the infinitive also belong to the first conjugation:

PERFECTIVE FUTURE

ВЕРНУ́ТЬ	TO RETURN, TO GIVE BACK
я верну́	I will return
ты вернёшь	you will return
он вернёт	he will return
мы вернём	we will return
вы вернёте	you will return
они́ верну́т	they will return

[1] С changes to ш, and the ending becomes у in the first-person singular and third-person plural.

Second Conjugation

говори́ть	to talk, to speak
я говорю́	I talk
ты говори́шь	you talk
он говори́т	he talks
мы говори́м	we talk
вы говори́те	you talk
они́ говоря́т	they talk

ви́деть[1]	to see
я ви́жу	I see
ты ви́дишь	you see
он ви́дит	he sees
мы ви́дим	we see
вы ви́дите	you see
они ви́дят	they see

звони́ть	to call, to ring
я звоню́	I call
ты звони́шь	you call
он звони́т	he calls
мы звони́м	we call
вы звони́те	you call
они́ звоня́т	they call

[1] Д changes to ж in the first person.

Mixed Conjugation

хоте́ть	to want
я хочу́	I want
ты хо́чешь	you want
он хо́чет	he wants
мы хоти́м	we want
вы хоти́те	you want
они́ хотя́т	they want

This verb in the singular has first-conjugation endings and changes the т to ч. In the plural it has second conjugation endings.

Reflexive Verbs

Verbs ending in -сь or -ся are reflexive, with -ся usually coming after a consonant and -сь coming after a vowel. These verbs follow the general conjugation form, retaining the -ся ending after consonants and -сь after vowels:

занима́ться	to study
я занима́юсь	I study
ты занима́ешься	you study
он занима́ется	he studies
мы занима́емся	we study
вы занима́етесь	you study
они́ занима́ются	they study

B. To Be or Not To Be: Быть

1. I am

The verb *to be* is usually omitted in the present tense:

Я до́ма.	I am at home.
Мой дом о́чень удо́бный	My home is very comfortable.

2. I was and I will be

However, *to be* is used in the past and future tenses:

Он был	he was
она́ была́	she was
оно́ бы́ло	it was
они́ бы́ли	they were
Я был до́ма.	I was at home.
Мо́й дом был удо́бный.	My home was comfortable.
я бу́ду	I will be
ты бу́дешь	you will be
он бу́дет	he will be
мы бу́дем	we will be
вы бу́дете	you will be
они́ бу́дут	they will be
Я бу́ду до́ма за́втра.	I will be home tomorrow.
Мой но́вый дом бу́дет о́чень удо́бный.	My new house will be very comfortable.

3. "To Be" as an Auxiliary

Быть (to be) is also used as an auxiliary verb in the imperfective future:

я бу́ду	I will
ты бу́дешь чита́ть	you will read
он бу́дет говори́ть	he will talk
мы бу́дем писа́ть	we will write
вы бу́дете etc.	you will etc.
они́ бу́дут	they will

C. The Past Tense

The past tense agrees with the gender of its subject. It is formed by dropping -ть from the infinitive and adding:

Masc.	**-л**	**он чита́л**	he was reading
Fem.	**-ла**	**она́ говори́ла**	she was speaking
Neut.	**-ло**	**пальто́ висе́ло**	the coat was hanging
Plur.	**-ли**	**они́ звони́ли**	they were calling

D. Word Study

и́мя	name
получа́ть-получи́ть	to receive
до́лго	for a long time
приве́т	greeting
за́втра	tomorrow
знамени́тый	famous
гро́мко	loudly
вре́мя	time
бога́тый	rich
коне́чно	of course

LESSON 14

A. Have and Have Not

Есть у вас маши́на?	Do you have a car?
У неё нет маши́ны.	She doesn't have a car.
У меня́ есть каранда́ш.	I have a pencil.
У меня́ нет каранда́ша́.	I don't have a pencil.
Есть у тебя́ газе́та?	Do you have a newspaper?
У тебя́ нет газе́ты.	You don't have a newspaper.
У него́ есть жена́ и сын.	He has a wife and a son.
У неё нет му́жа.	She doesn't have a husband.
У нас нет де́нег.	We don't have (any) money.
У вас есть ка́рта Москвы́?	Do you have a map of Moscow?
У вас нет ка́рты Москвы́.	You don't have a map of Moscow.
У них нет вре́мени.	They don't have time.
У меня́ есть вре́мя.	I have time.
У меня́ нет вре́мени.	I don't have time.
Вот хоро́ший магази́н; у них есть всё, что вам ну́жно.	Here's a good store; they have everything you need.
Вот мой друг.	Here is my friend.
У него́ нет друзе́й.	He has no friends.
У вас есть сигаре́ты?	Do you have cigarettes?

У меня́ нет спи́чек.	I don't have (any) matches.
У кого́ есть спи́чки?	Who has matches?

NOTE

1. In Russian, possession is usually expressed by the following form:

у меня́ есть	I have [by me is/are]
у тебя́ есть	you have [by you is/are *fam.*]
у него́ есть	he has [by him is/are]
у неё есть	she has [by her is/are]
у нас есть	we have [by us is/are]
у вас есть	you have [by you is/are *pl.* and *pol. sing.*]
у них есть	they have [by them is/are]

2. When the negative is used, the object of the negative is in the genitive case:

У меня́ нет карандаша́	I do not have a pencil. [By me is not a pencil.]
У вас нет сестры́.	You do not have a sister. [By you is not a sister.]

3. If you want to know if someone has the thing you are looking for or the thing you need, use the word есть. However, if you want to know who has something you know is there, then omit the verb есть.

B. To Want and To Feel Like

These are impersonal verb forms and adverb forms with the dative:

1. "To want" is expressed by the verb хоте́ть.

2. "To feel like" is expressed by the reflexive verb хо́чется with the dative case:

Он хо́чет есть.	He is hungry. [He wants to eat.]
Я хочу́ пить.	I want a (to) drink.
Мне хо́чется . . .	I feel like [to me it is wanting] . . .
Мне хо́чется пить.	I'm thirsty. [I feel like drinking.]
Мы хоти́м чита́ть.	We want to read.
Они́ хотя́т спать.	They want to sleep.
Мне хо́чется спать.	I feel like sleeping.
Ему́ хо́чется есть.	He feels like eating.
Им хо́чется пойти́ в кино́.	They feel like going to the movies.

3. The same form and construction are used with the following verbs:

нра́виться	to please, to like
каза́ться	to seem
Мне нра́вится э́тот го́род.	I like this city. [To me is pleasing this city.]
Мне ка́жется, что я вас зна́ю.	It seems to me that I know you. [To me it seems, etc.]

4. The same form and construction are used with the following adverbs:

хо́лодно	cold
жа́рко	hot
тепло́	warm
прия́тно	pleasant
легко́	easy
интере́сно	interesting
стра́нно	strange

Мне хо́лодно.	I am cold. [To me it is cold.]
Ему́ жа́рко.	He is hot. [To him it is hot.]
Ей тепло́.	She is warm. [To her it is warm.]
Мне прия́тно.	It's nice/ pleasant. [To me it is pleasant.]
Нам легко́.	It is easy for us. [To us it is easy.]
Мне интере́сно.	I am interested. [To me it is interesting.]

C. Personal Pronouns with Prepositions

All forms of personal pronouns beginning with vowels take the letter н when used with prepositions:

у него́ есть	he has
Мы зашли́ к нему́.	We went to see him.
Я рабо́тала с ни́ми.	I worked with them.

However, when его́, её and их are employed as adjectives, they do not take the н when used with prepositions:

у его́ бра́та есть	his brother has
Мы зашли́ в их но́вый дом.	We went to their new house.
Она́ пришла́ с её сестро́й.	She came with her sister.

QUIZ 5

1. У него́ есть машина.	a. They have no time.
2. Ей здесь хо́лодно.	b. I feel like sleeping.
3. Вот моя́ кни́га.	c. He doesn't have a wife.
4. У них нет вре́мени.	d. This is their son.
5. Э́то их сын.	e. It's hot here.
6. Мне хо́чется спать.	f. She is cold here.
7. Тут жа́рко.	g. Who has matches?
8. Э́то о́чень далеко́.	h. Here is my book.
9. У него́ нет жены́.	i. He has a car.
10. У кого́ есть спи́чки?	j. It's very far.

ANSWERS

1—i; 2—f; 3—h; 4—a; 5—d; 6—b; 7—e; 8—j; 9—c; 10—g.

LESSON 15

A. Do You Speak Russian?

A general (yes/no) question in Russian is expressed mostly by intonation, not by any particular construction of the sentence. "Do you speak Russian?" in Russian is Вы говори́те по-ру́сски? [You speak by-Russian?] The answer is: Говорю́ (Speak.) You do not have to use the pronoun *I* (я), since the ending of the verb говорю́ indicates the first person singular. Other questions in Russian are formed with the help of question words (see Lessons 16 and 17).

Вы говори́те по-ру́сски?	Do you speak Russian?
Да, немно́го.	Yes, a little.
Не о́чень хорошо́.	Not very well.

Я говорю́ по-ру́сски.	I speak Russian.
Он говори́т по-англи́йски.	He speaks English.
Я говорю́ о́чень пло́хо.	I speak very badly.
Мы говори́м по-ру́сски о́чень ме́дленно.	We speak Russian very slowly.
Я зна́ю то́лько не́сколько слов.	I know only a few words.
Я могу́ сказа́ть то́лько не́сколько слов по-ру́сски.	I can say only a few words in Russian.
Ваш дру́г говори́т по-ру́сски?	Does your friend speak Russian?
Нет, не говори́т.	No, he doesn't.
Вы понима́ете по-ру́сски?	Do you understand Russian?
Да, понима́ю.	Yes, I understand (it).
Да, понима́ю, но не говорю́.	Yes, I understand but don't speak (it).
Я чита́ю, но не говорю́.	I read but do not speak (it).
Они́ понима́ют по-ру́сски о́чень хорошо́.	They understand Russian very well.
Вы пло́хо произно́сите ру́сские слова́.	You pronounce Russian words badly.
Э́то о́чень тру́дное сло́во.	That's a very difficult word.
Мне нужна́ пра́ктика.	I need practice.
Вы понима́ете меня́?	Do you understand me?

Да, я вас понима́ю.	Yes, I understand you.
Нет, я вас не понима́ю.	No, I don't understand you.
Что вы сказа́ли?	What did you say?
Вы говори́те сли́шком бы́стро.	You speak too fast.
Не говори́те так бы́стро.	Don't talk so fast.
Мне тру́дно понима́ть, когда́ вы говори́те так бы́стро.	It's difficult for me to understand when you speak so fast.
Говори́те ме́дленнее.	Speak more slowly.
Пожа́луйста, говори́те немно́го ме́дленнее.	Please speak a little more slowly.
Прости́те, но я не понима́ю вас.	Excuse me, but I don't understand you.
Пожа́луйста, повтори́те.	Please repeat.
Вы понима́ете меня́ тепе́рь?	Do you understand me now?
Да, тепе́рь я понима́ю.	Yes, now I understand.
Я хочу́ хорошо́ говори́ть по-ру́сски.	I want to speak Russian well.
Вы говори́те по-англи́йски?	Do you speak English?

B. The Weather

Кака́я сего́дня пого́да?	What's the weather today?

Идёт дождь.	It's raining.
Идёт снег.	It's snowing.
Сейча́с хо́лодно.	It's cold.
Сейча́с па́смурно.	It's cloudy.
Сейча́с тепло́	It's warm.
Сейча́с прия́тно.	It's nice.
Сейча́с жа́рко.	It's hot.
Сейча́с со́лнечно.	It's sunny.
Сейча́с ве́трено.	It's windy.
Како́й прогно́з на за́втра?	What's the forecast for tomorrow?

C. Word Study

ве́жливый	polite
бе́дный	poor
брать-взять	to take
дорого́й	expensive, dear
жизнь	life
ве́чер	evening
весёлый	cheerful
ско́лько	how much
опя́ть	again
ма́ло	little
нау́ка	science

QUIZ 6

Fill in the blanks with the appropriate Russian word.

1. Вы _____ по-ру́сски? Do you speak Russian?
2. Я _____ но не _____. I understand, but don't speak.
3. _____ ме́дленнее. Speak more slowly.
4. Что вы _____? What did you say?
5. Я _____ то́лько не́сколько слов. I know only a few words.
6. Она́ _____ по-ру́сски о́чень _____. She reads

Russian very well.
7. Сейча́с _____. It's cold.
8. Не говори́те так _____. Don't talk so fast.
9. _____, но я вас не понима́ю. Excuse me, but I don't understand you.
10. Кака́я сего́дня _____? What's the weather today?

ANSWERS

1. говори́те; 2. понима́ю, говорю́; 3. Ґовори́те; 4. сказа́ли; 5. зна́ю; 6. чита́ет, хорошо́; 7. хо́лодно; 8. бы́стро; 9. Прости́те; 10. пого́да.

LESSON 16

A. What, Which, and Where

Кото́рый сейча́с час?	What time is it now?
В кото́ром часу́?	At what time?
Вот кни́га, кото́рую я чита́л.	Here is the book that I was reading.
Де́ло, кото́рое он на́чал, идёт хорошо́.	The business that he started is going well.
Како́й э́то краси́вый язы́к!	What a pretty language this is!
Кака́я сего́дня пого́да?	What kind of weather is it today?
Каку́ю кни́гу вы чита́ете?	What book are you reading?
О како́й кни́ге вы говори́ли?	What book were you talking about?
Како́е сего́дня число́?	What is the date today?

Како́е вино́ вы хоти́те: кра́сное и́ли бе́лое?	Which wine do you want: red or white?
Како́й он у́мный!	How clever he is!
Да́йте мне каку́ю-нибудь кни́гу.	Give me any book.
Како́й вы стра́нный челове́к!	What a strange person you are!
Кака́я она́ краси́вая де́вушка!	What a pretty girl she is!
Куда́ вы идёте?	Where are you going?
Я иду́ на рабо́ту.	I'm going to work.
Где ва́ша рабо́та?	Where do you work?
Я рабо́таю на Театра́льной пло́щади.	I work on Theatre Square.
Что на столе́?	What's on the table (location)?
На столе́ кни́ги, бума́га и каранда́ш.	Books, paper, and a pencil are on the table.
Куда́ вы положи́ли мою́ кни́гу?	Where did you put my book?
На стол.	On the table (direction).
Куда́ вы идёте обе́дать по́сле рабо́ты?	Where are you going to have dinner (to dine) after work?
Я иду́ домо́й.	I'm going home.
Я бу́ду обе́дать до́ма.	I will have dinner at home.
Отку́да вы?	Where are you from?
Я из Петербу́рга.	I'm from St. Petersburg.
Да что вы!	You don't say!
Я то́же отту́да.	I'm also from there.
Како́е совпаде́ние! Удиви́тельно!	What a coincidence! Amazing!

B. Which, What

кото́рый, кото́рая, кото́рое, кото́рые како́й, кака́я, како́е, каки́е	which, what

"Which" and "what" are declined like adjectives and must agree in gender, number, and case with the nouns they modify.

Како́й краси́вый дом!	What a pretty house!

Here дом is masculine, nominative, and singular; so is како́й.

На каку́ю карти́ну вы смо́трите?	Which picture are you looking at?

Карти́ну is feminine, accusative, and singular; so is каку́ю.

О каки́х кни́гах вы говори́ли?	Which books were you talking about?

Кни́гах is feminine, plural, and prepositional; so is каки́х.

C. Where with the Accusative and Prepositional

"Where" in Russian is rendered by:

Куда́ "where to," "whither" (direction) is always used with the accusative case.

Где "where is" (location) is always used with the prepositional case.

Я иду́ в шко́лу.	I go to school.
идти́ в шко́лу	to go to (direction)
Я рабо́таю в шко́ле.	I work in (the) school.
рабо́тать в шко́ле	to work in (location)
Кни́гу положи́ли на стол.	They put the book on the table.
положи́ть на стол	to put on (direction)
Кни́га лежи́т на столе́.	The book is lying on the table.
лежа́ть на столе́	to lie on (location)

QUIZ 7

1. _____ э́то краси́вый язы́к! What a pretty language this is!
2. _____ вы идёте по́сле рабо́ты? Where are you going after work?
3. _____ вы рабо́таете? Where do you work?
4. _____ вы положи́ли мою́ кни́гу? Where did you put my book?
5. О _____ кни́ге вы говори́те? What book you are talking about?
6. Кни́га, _____ я чита́ю, о́чень хоро́шая. The book which I am reading is very good.
7. Я положи́л её _____. I put it on the table.
8. Да́йте мне _____ кни́гу. Give me any book.
9. _____ она́ у́мная! How clever she is!
10. _____ э́то краси́вое пальто́! What a beautiful coat this is!

ANSWERS

1. Како́й; 2. Куда́; 3. Где; 4. Куда́; 5. како́й; 6. кото́рую; 7. на стол; 8. каку́ю-нибудь; 9. Кака́я; 10. Како́е.

LESSON 17

A. Whose?

Чей э́то дом?	Whose house is that?
Чей э́то карандáш?	Whose pencil is that?
Чья э́то кни́га?	Whose book is that?
Чья газéта там на столé?	Whose newspaper is [there] on the table?
Чьё э́то пальтó?	Whose coat is that?
Чьи э́ти дéти?	Whose children are these?
Чьи дéньги онá трáтит?	Whose money does she spend?

Чей, чья, чьё, чьи (whose) agree in gender, number, and case with nouns they modify:

Чья кни́га?	Whose book?

Кни́га is feminine and nominative; so is чья.

На чью кни́гу вы смóтрите?	Whose book are you looking at?

Кни́гу is feminine and accusative; so is чью.

Чьим карандашóм вы пи́шете?	Whose pencil are you writing with?

Карандашóм is masculine and instrumental; so is чьим.

	Masc.	Fem.	Neut.	Plur. All Gend.
Nom.	чей	чья	чьё	чьи
Gen.	чьего́	чьей	чьего́	чьих
Dat.	чьему́	чьей	чьему́	чьим
Acc.	Same as nom. or gen.	чью	чьё	Same as nom. or gen.
Inst.	чьим	чьей(е́ю)	чьим	чьи́ми
Prep.	о чьём	о чьей	о чьём	о чьих

B. What, How

Как вас зову́т? — What is your name? [How are you called?]

Как ва́ше и́мя? — What is your name?

Как её зову́т? — What is her name?

Как дела́? — How are things?

Как по-ру́сски . . . ? — What is the Russian for . . . ?

Как э́то пи́шется? — How is that spelled?

Как называ́ется э́та кни́га? — What is the name of this book?

Как называ́ется э́тот го́род? — What is the name of this city?

Как пройти́ на у́лицу Го́рького? — How do you get to Gorky Street?

Как вы ду́маете, он хорошо́ говори́т по-ру́сски? — What do you think, does he speak Russian well?

Как хорошо́ он говори́т по-ру́сски! — How well he speaks Russian!

Как здесь жа́рко! — How hot it is here!

Как вам нра́вится Москва́?	How do you like Moscow?
Как вам не сты́дно так бы́стро забы́ть меня́!	Aren't you ashamed to have forgotten me so quickly?
Как я ра́да, что встре́тила вас!	How glad I am that I met you!
Вот как!	Is that so!
Как прия́тно гуля́ть в саду́!	How pleasant it is to stroll in the garden!
Как ни стара́йтесь– ничего́ не вы́йдет.	No matter how you try, nothing will come of it.
Как бы не так!	Nothing of the sort!
Бу́дьте как до́ма.	Make yourself at home.
с тех пор, как	since
как ви́дно	apparently [as it is seen]
Э́то как раз то, что мне ну́жно!	It's just the thing I need!

C. The Demonstrative Pronoun Э́то

Note the difference between: э́то, meaning "this is," "that is," and э́тот, э́та, э́то, meaning "this."

Э́то каранда́ш.	This is a pencil.
Э́тот каранда́ш мой.	This pencil is mine.
Э́то кни́га.	This is a book.
Э́та кни́га не моя́.	This book is not mine.

D. Word Study

переводи́ть-перевести́	to translate
симпати́чный	nice

о́коло	near
фотогра́фия	photograph
коне́ц	end
изуча́ть-изучи́ть	to study in depth
тёплый	warm
ве́тер	wind
страна́	country
доро́га	road

QUIZ 8

1. Как называ́ется э́тот го́род?
2. Как вам не сты́дно так ско́ро забы́ть меня́?
3. Как дела́?
4. Бу́дьте как до́ма.
5. Как бы не так!
6. Чьи э́ти де́ти?
7. Чей э́то каранда́ш?
8. Как прия́тно гуля́ть в саду́!
9. Как вас зову́т?
10. Как э́то пи́шется?
11. Как здесь жа́рко!
12. Как дойти́ до у́лицы Го́рького?
13. Чей э́то дом?
14. Вот как!
15. Как по-ру́сски . . . ?
16. Как называ́ется э́та кни́га?
17. Как я рад, что встре́тил вас!
18. Как вы ду́маете, он хорошо́ говори́т по-ру́сски?

a. How pleasant it is to stroll in the garden!
b. What is the Russian for . . . ?
c. Make yourself at home.
d. Whose children are these?
e. How hot it is here!
f. What is your name?
g. Whose house is this?
h. How do you get to Gorky Street?
i. Is that so!
j. What is the name of this city?
k. How are things?
l. Whose pencil is that?
m. What is the name of this book?
n. Aren't you ashamed to have forgotten me so soon?
o. How glad I am that I met you!
p. What do you think, does he speak Russian well?
q. How is that spelled?
r. Nothing of the sort!

ANSWERS

1—j; 2—n; 3—k; 4—c; 5—r; 6—d; 7—l; 8—a; 9—f; 10—q; 11—e; 12—h; 13—g; 14—i; 15—b; 16—m; 17—o; 18—p.

LESSON 18

A. Meeting a Friend

До́брое у́тро.	Good morning.
Здра́вствуйте.	Hello.
Вы говори́те по-ру́сски?	Do you speak Russian?
Да, я говорю́ по-ру́сски.	Yes, I speak Russian.
А я не говорю́ по-англи́йски.	And I don't speak English.
Вы с ю́га?	Are you from the south?
Да, я из Кры́ма.	Yes, I'm from the Crimea.
Как давно́ (or ско́лько вре́мени) **вы уже́ в Соединённых Шта́тах?**	How long (how much time) have you been in the United States?
Два ме́сяца.	Two months.
Вы бы́стро вы́учите англи́йский язы́к.	You will learn English quickly.
Э́тот язы́к не о́чень тру́дный.	This language is not very difficult.
Он гора́здо трудне́е, чем вы ду́маете.	It's far more difficult than you think.
Возмо́жно, вы пра́вы. Наве́рно, нам гора́здо ле́гче вы́учить ру́сский язы́к, чем вам вы́учить англи́йский.	You may be right. It's probably much easier for us to learn Russian than for you to learn English.
Вы говори́те по-ру́сски о́чень хорошо́.	You speak Russian very well.
Я жил в Крыму́ не́сколько лет.	I lived in the Crimea for several years.

У вас прекра́сное произноше́ние.	Your pronunciation is excellent. [You have excellent pronunciation.]
Спаси́бо, но всё же мне ну́жно бо́льше говори́ть (or мне нужна́ пра́ктика).	Thank you, but all the same I need to speak more (I need practice).
Мне ну́жно идти́. Мой по́езд ско́ро отхо́дит.	I have to go. My train is leaving soon.
Всего́ хоро́шего и счастли́вого пути́.	All the best, and have a pleasant trip.
Жела́ю и вам того́ же. До свида́ния.	The same to you. Good-bye.
До свида́ния.	Good-bye.

QUIZ 9

Choose the correct word:

1. Она́ _____ (speaks) по-ру́сски.
   a. говорю́
   b. чита́ет
   c. говори́т

2. Я _____ (don't speak) по-англи́йски.
   a. чита́ю
   b. не говорю́
   c. говори́т

3. Я _____ (lived) в Крыму́.
   a. рабо́таю
   b. жить
   c. жил

4. Ру́сский _____ (easier) чем англи́йский.
   a. ле́гче
   b. бо́льше
   c. хорошо́

5. Кака́я _____ (today) пого́да?
   a. за́втра
   b. вчера́
   c. сего́дня

6. Как называ́ется э́тот _____ (city)?
   a. кни́га
   b. го́род
   c. у́лица

7. Я иду́ _____ (home).
   a. до́ма
   b. домо́й
   c. в до́ме

8. Куда́ вы _____ (are going)?
   a. иду́
   b. идёт
   c. идёте

9. _____ (What) сего́дня число́?
   a. Како́е
   b. Что
   c. Как

10. _____ (Which) тепе́рь час?
   a. Како́е
   b. Кото́рый
   c. Каку́ю

11. _____ (Where) вы́ рабо́таете?
   a. Где
   b. Куда́
   c. Как

12. _____ (Where) вы положи́ли кни́гу?
   a. Где
   b. Куда́
   c. Как

13. Вы говори́те сли́шком _____ (fast).
   a. пло́хо
   b. бы́стро
   c. ти́хо

14. Я _____ (you) не понима́ю.
    a. вам
    b. вы
    c. вас

15. _____ (he has) нет друзе́й.
    a. У него́
    b. У меня́
    c. У вас

16. _____ (She has) нет му́жа.
    a. У меня́
    b. У неё
    c. У него́

17. _____ (I am) хо́лодно.
    a. Мне
    b. Ему́
    c. Вам

18. _____ (She is) жа́рко.
    a. Мне
    b. Ей
    c. Её

19. Вот _____ (good) магази́н.
    a. хоро́ший
    b. до́брый
    c. плохо́й

20. Они́ _____ (want) спать.
    a. хочу́
    b. хо́чешь
    c. хотя́т

ANSWERS

1—c; 2—b; 3—c; 4—a; 5—c; 6—b; 7—b; 8—c; 9—a; 10—b; 11—a; 12—b; 13—b; 14—c; 15—a; 16—b; 17—a; 18—b; 19—a; 20—c.

B. Introductions

1. Pleased to Meet You

Разреши́те предста́виться.	Allow me to introduce myself.
Меня́ зову́т Ива́н.	My name is John.
Меня́ зову́т Мари́я.	My name is Mary.
О́чень прия́тно.	Pleased to meet you.
Я хоте́ла бы предста́вить вас И́горю.	I'd like to introduce you to Igor.
Отку́да вы?	Where are you from?
Я живу́ в США.	I live in the U.S.
Я живу́ в А́нглии.	I live in England.
Я в командиро́вке.	I'm here on a business trip.

2. Are You Here on Vacation?

До́брый день!	Hello!
Разреши́те предста́виться. Меня́ зову́т Дже́йн Бра́ун.	Allow me to introduce myself. My name is Jane Brown.
О́чень прия́тно с ва́ми познако́миться.	Pleased to meet you.
Меня́ зову́т Ива́н Семёнов.	My name is Ivan Semyonov.
О́чень прия́тно.	Pleased to meet you.
Вы здесь в отпуску́?	Are you here on vacation?
Да. Я бу́ду в Москве́ ещё четы́ре дня.	Yes. I'll be here in Moscow another four days.
Жела́ю вам прия́тно провести́ вре́мя!	Have a pleasant time!

C. Word Study

совреме́нный	contemporary
нача́ло	beginning
портре́т	portrait
пра́вильно	correctly
люби́ть	to love
везде́	everywhere
рад	glad (adj.)
тру́дный	difficult
мир	world, peace

LESSON 19

A. Cardinal Numerals

оди́н	one
два	two
три	three
четы́ре	four
пять	five
шесть	six
семь	seven
во́семь	eight
де́вять	nine
де́сять	ten
оди́ннадцать	eleven
двена́дцать	twelve
трина́дцать	thirteen
четы́рнадцать	fourteen
пятна́дцать	fifteen
шестна́дцать	sixteen
семна́дцать	seventeen

восемна́дцать	eighteen
девятна́дцать	nineteen
два́дцать	twenty
два́дцать оди́н	twenty-one
два́дцать два	twenty-two
два́дцать три	twenty-three
три́дцать	thirty
три́дцать оди́н	thirty-one
три́дцать два	thirty-two
три́дцать три	thirty-three
со́рок	forty
со́рок оди́н	forty-one
со́рок два	forty-two
со́рок три	forty-three
пятьдеся́т	fifty
пятьдеся́т оди́н	fifty-one
пятьдеся́т два	fifty-two
пятьдеся́т три	fifty-three
шестьдеся́т	sixty
шестьдеся́т оди́н	sixty-one
шестьдеся́т два	sixty-two
шестьдеся́т три	sixty-three
се́мьдесят	seventy
се́мьдесят оди́н	seventy-one
се́мьдесят два	seventy-two
се́мьдесят три	seventy-three
во́семьдесят	eighty
во́семьдесят оди́н	eighty-one
во́семьдесят два	eighty-two
во́семьдесят три	eighty-three
девяно́сто	ninety
девяно́сто оди́н	ninety-one
девяно́сто два	ninety-two
девяно́сто три	ninety-three
сто	one hundred

сто оди́н	one hundred one
сто два	one hundred two
сто три	one hundred three
сто два́дцать	one hundred twenty
сто три́дцать	one hundred thirty
сто три́дцать оди́н	one hundred thirty-one
сто три́дцать два	one hundred thirty-two
сто три́дцать три	one hundred thirty-three
две́сти	two hundred
три́ста	three hundred
четы́реста	four hundred
пятьсо́т	five hundred
шестьсо́т	six hundred
семьсо́т	seven hundred
восемьсо́т	eight hundred
девятьсо́т	nine hundred
ты́сяча	one thousand
миллио́н	one million
миллиа́рд	one billion

B. Cases with Cardinal Numerals

оди́н (*m*), одна́ (*f.*), одно́ (*n.*), одни́ (*pl.*)
два (*m.*), две (*f.*), два (*n.*)

1. When the cardinal numeral is used in the nominative case:

The nominative singular is used after оди́н, одна́, одно́.
The nominative plural is used after одни́.
The genitive singular is used after два, две, три, четы́ре.
The genitive plural is used after пять, шесть, семь, etc.

2. When the number is compound, the case of the noun depends on the last digit:

Sing.	два́дцать оди́н каранда́ш	twenty-one pencils
Gen. *Sing.*	два́дцать два каранда́ша́	twenty-two pencils
Gen. *Pl.*	два́дцать пять каранда́ше́й	twenty-five pencils

C. Declension of Numerals

All cardinal numerals decline, agreeing with the noun they quantify, with the following exceptions:

a. When the noun is in the nominative case (as discussed above).
b. When the numeral is 2–4 in the accusative case (or a compound ending in 2–4) and the noun is inanimate, then the noun is in its genitive singular form.
c. When the numeral is 5–20 in the accusative case (or a compound ending in 5–20) then the noun is in its genitive plural form.

Gen. *Sing.*	**Я прочита́ла два письма́.** I read two letters.
Gen *Pl.*	**Он был там оди́н ме́сяц без двух дней.** He was there one month less two days.
Dat. *Pl.*	**Мы пришли́ к пяти́ часа́м.** We arrived by five o'clock.
Prep. *Pl.*	**Они́ говоря́т о семи́ людях.** They are speaking about seven people.

Declension of Numerals

	Singular one			Plural only (all genders)
	Masc.	Fem.	Neut.	
Nom.	оди́н	одна́	одно́	одни́
Gen.	одного́	одно́й	одного́	одни́х
Dat.	одному́	одно́й	одному́	одни́м
Acc.	Same as nom. or gen.	одну́	одно́	Same as nom. or gen.
Inst.	одни́м	одно́й(-о́ю)	одни́м	одни́ми
Prep.	об одно́м	об одно́й	об одно́м	об одни́х

	two	three	four	five
Nom.	два, две	три	четы́ре	пять
Gen.	двух	трёх	четырёх	пяти́
Dat.	двум	трём	четырём	пяти́
Acc.	Same as nom. or gen.	Same as nom. or gen.	Same as nom. or gen.	пять
Inst.	двумя́	тремя́	четырьмя́	пятью́
Prep.	о двух	о трёх	о четырёх	о пяти́

NOTE

All numbers from 6 to 20 follow the same declension pattern as 5.

QUIZ 10

1. Де́вять	a. 102
2. Два́дцать оди́н	b. 43
3. Двена́дцать	c. 600
4. Пятьдеся́т	d. 30
5. Пятна́дцать	e. 1,000
6. Со́рок три	f. 5
7. Четы́рнадцать	g. 9
8. Четы́реста	h. 15
9. Сто два	i. 50
10. Пять	j. 11
11. Шестьсо́т	k. 21
12. Ты́сяча	l. 80
13. Три́дцать	m. 400
14. Оди́ннадцать	n. 14
15. Во́семьдесят	o. 12

ANSWERS

1—g; 2—k; 3—o; 4—i; 5—h; 6—b; 7—n; 8—m; 9—a; 10—f; 11—c; 12—e; 13—d; 14—j; 15—l.

LESSON 20

A. Ordinal Numbers

пе́рвый	first
второ́й	second
тре́тий	third
четвёртый	fourth
пя́тый	fifth
шесто́й	sixth
седьмо́й	seventh
восьмо́й	eighth
девя́тый	ninth
деся́тый	tenth
оди́ннадцатый	eleventh
двена́дцатый	twelfth
трина́дцатый	thirteenth
четы́рнадцатый	fourteenth
пятна́дцатый	fifteenth
шестна́дцатый	sixteenth
семна́дцатый	seventeenth
восемна́дцатый	eighteenth
девятна́дцатый	nineteenth
двадца́тый	twentieth
два́дцать пе́рвый	twenty-first
два́дцать второ́й	twenty-second
два́дцать тре́тий	twenty-third
тридца́тый	thirtieth
три́дцать пе́рвый	thirty-first
три́дцать второ́й	thirty-second
три́дцать тре́тий	thirty-third
сороково́й	fortieth
со́рок пе́рвый	forty-first
со́рок второ́й	forty-second
со́рок тре́тий	forty-third
пятидеся́тый	fiftieth

пятьдеся́т пе́рвый	fifty-first
пятьдеся́т второ́й	fifty-second
пятьдеся́т тре́тий	fifty-third
шестидеся́тый	sixtieth
шестьдеся́т пе́рвый	sixty-first
шестьдеся́т второ́й	sixty-second
шестьдеся́т тре́тий	sixty-third
семидеся́тый	seventieth
се́мьдесят пе́рвый	seventy-first
се́мьдесят второ́й	seventy-second
се́мьдесят тре́тий	seventy-third
восьмидеся́тый	eightieth
во́семьдесят пе́рвый	eighty-first
во́семьдесят второ́й	eighty-second
во́семьдесят тре́тий	eighty-third
девяно́стый	ninetieth
девяно́сто пе́рвый	ninety-first
девяно́сто второ́й	ninety-second
девяно́сто тре́тий	ninety-third
со́тый	hundredth
сто пе́рвый	hundred first
сто второ́й	hundred second
сто тре́тий	hundred third
сто двадца́тый	hundred twentieth
сто тридца́тый	hundred thirtieth
сто три́дцать пе́рвый	hundred thirty-first
сто три́дцать второ́й	hundred thirty-second
сто три́дцать тре́тий	hundred thirty-third
двухсо́тый	two hundredth
трёхсо́тый*	three hundredth
четырёхсо́тый*	four hundredth
пятисо́тый	five hundredth
шестисо́тый	six hundredth

* These are two of the very few exceptions where one word has two stresses, and that is only because they are compound words.

семисо́тый	seven hundredth
восьмисо́тый	eight hundredth
девятисо́тый	nine hundredth
ты́сячный	thousandth
миллио́нный	millionth
миллиа́рдный	billionth

B. Characteristics of Ordinal Numerals

All ordinal numerals are like adjectives, and decline as such:

Masc.	Fem.	Neut.	Plur.
пе́рвый второ́й	пе́рвая втора́я	пе́рвое второ́е	пе́рвые вторы́е

In compound forms, only the last digit changes, and only that digit is declined:

двадца́тый век	twentieth century
Это бы́ло три́дцать пе́рвого декабря́.	That was on December 31.
тре́тий раз	third time
Втора́я мирова́я война́ ко́нчилась в ты́сяча девятьсо́т со́рок пя́том году́.	The Second World War ended in 1945 [one thousand, nine hundred, forty-fifth year].

пя́тый год
пя́том году́ (prepositional singular)

C. Word Study

река́	river
кли́мат	climate
рома́н	novel
находи́ться	to be located
висе́ть	to be hanging
расска́з	story
давно́	a long time ago
холо́дный	cold
чай	tea
господи́н	Mister

LESSON 21

A. Numbers in Context

Это двадца́тый уро́к.	This is the twentieth lesson.
Я уже́ зна́ю девятна́дцать уро́ков.	I already know nineteen lessons.
Я купи́ла но́вую шля́пу за ты́сячу рубле́й.	I bought a new hat for a thousand rubles.
Ско́лько вам лет?	How old are you?
Мне два́дцать лет.	I am twenty years old.
Ему́ два́дцать оди́н год.	He is twenty-one years old.
Ей три́дцать два го́да.	She is thirty-two years old.

Ива́ну Петро́вичу три́дцать пять лет.	Ivan Petrovich is thirty-five years old.
Я встаю́ в во́семь часо́в утра́.	I get up at eight o'clock in the morning.
Он рабо́тает с девяти́ утра́ до пяти́ часо́в ве́чера.	He works from nine in the morning until five [o'clock] in the evening.
Ско́лько сто́ит биле́т?	How much does a ticket cost?
(Биле́т сто́ит) **сто пятьдеся́т рубле́й.**	(A ticket costs) one hundred and fifty rubles.
Ско́лько сто́ит э́та руба́шка?	How much does this shirt cost?
(Э́та руба́шка сто́ит) **ты́сяча и пятьсо́т рубле́й.**	This shirt costs one thousand five hundred rubles.
Э́то о́чень до́рого.	That's very expensive.
Э́то дёшево.	That's cheap.
Да́йте мне, пожа́луйста, друго́й.	Please give me another [a different one].
Покажи́те мне, пожа́луйста, э́ту кни́гу.	Please show me this book.
Каку́ю? Э́ту?	Which one? This one?
Нет, не э́ту, а ту другу́ю.	No, not this, but that one.
Пожа́луйста.	Please.
Ско́лько она́ сто́ит?	How much does it cost?
Четы́реста три́дцать семь рубле́й.	Four hundred thirty-seven rubles.
Э́то не до́рого.	That's not expensive.
Я куплю́ её.	I'll buy it.
Когда́ я прие́хала в Москву́, я обменя́ла две́сти до́лларов.	When I arrived in Moscow, I exchanged two hundred dollars.

В э́той гости́нице де́вять этаже́й.	There are nine floors in this hotel.
Мой друг живёт на у́лице Пу́шкина, дом но́мер сто во́семьдесят четы́ре, кварти́ра два́дцать три.	My friend lives at 184 Pushkin Street, Apartment 23. [My friend lives on Pushkin street, house number one hundred eighty-four, apartment twenty-three.]
Его́ телефо́н 217-34-57.	His telephone number is 217-34-57.
Мой телефо́н 6-71-85.	My telephone number is 6-71-85.

B. How Old Are You?

"How old are you?" is expressed in Russian by the phrase Ско́лько вам (dative of вы) лет? [How many to you of years (of summers)?]

Мне два́дцать лет.	I am twenty years old. [To me twenty years.]

After 20, use the genitive plural.

Мне со́рок пять лет.	I am forty-five years old. [To me forty-five years.]

After 5, use the genitive plural.

Ему́ три́дцать оди́н год.	He is thirty-one years old. [To him thirty-one years.]

After 1, use the nominative singular.

Ей два́дцать три го́да.	She is twenty-three years old. [To her twenty-three years.]

After 3, use the genitive singular.

C. How Much, How Many

"How much?" and "how many?" are both expressed by one word in Russian: ско́лько.

Ско́лько э́то сто́ит?	How much does it cost?
Ско́лько раз я вам э́то говори́ла?	How many times have I told you that?
Ско́лько ученико́в в кла́ссе?	How many students are in the class?

After ско́лько and other adverbs of quantity—не́сколько (several), мно́го (many), ма́ло (little)—the genitive plural is always used. If, however, the noun denotes an uncountable entity, such as вре́мя (time), вода́ (water) or вино́ (wine), the genitive singular is used.

QUIZ 11

1. Я купи́л но́вую шля́пу за _____ рубле́й. I bought a new hat for forty thousand rubles.
2. Ей _____ го́да. She is thirty-two years old.
3. Я встаю́ в _____ часо́в утра́. I get up at eight o'clock in the morning.
4. У меня́ есть _____ до́лларов. I have two hundred dollars.
5. _____ сто́ит э́тот костю́м? How much does this suit cost?

6. _____ книг вы взя́ли домо́й? How many books did you take home?
7. Мой друг _____ на у́лице Пу́шкина. My friend lives on Pushkin Street.
8. Дом но́мер _____, кварти́ра _____. [House] Number 184, Apartment 23.
9. В э́той гости́нице _____ этаже́й. There are nine floors in this hotel.
10. Он рабо́тает с _____ утра́ до _____ ве́чера. He works from nine in the morning until five [o'clock] in the evening.

ANSWERS

1. со́рок ты́сяч; 2. три́дцать два; 3. во́семь; 4. две́сти; 5. Ско́лько; 6. Ско́лько; 7. живёт; 8. сто во́семьдесят четы́ре, два́дцать три; 9. де́вять; 10. девяти́, пяти́.

LESSON 22

A. I Like, I Don't Like

Мне о́чень нра́вится э́тот го́род.	I like this city very much.
Мне не нра́вится э́та у́лица.	I don't like this street.
Я люблю́ жить в дере́вне ле́том.	I love to live in the country during the summer.
В Нью-Йо́рке есть мно́го хоро́ших рестора́нов.	There are many good restaurants in New York.
Мне не нра́вится э́тот рестора́н.	I don't like this restaurant.
Како́й вку́сный ко́фе!	What delicious coffee!
Я всегда́ пью ко́фе с молоко́м.	I always drink coffee with milk.

Я не люблю́ молоко́.	I don't like milk.
Ко́фе без молока́ гора́здо вкусне́е.	Coffee without milk tastes much better [is much tastier].
Э́то де́ло вку́са.	It's a question of taste.
Како́е вку́сное пиро́жное!	What delicious pastry.
Переда́йте, мне, пожа́луйста, са́хар, соль, ло́жку, нож, ви́лку, хлеб.	Please pass [me] the sugar, salt, spoon, knife, fork, [and] bread.
Где моя́ салфе́тка?	Where is my napkin?

B. Telling Time

Telling time in Russian is rather complicated, but the simple form—два пятна́дцать (2:15), пять со́рок пять (5:45)—may always be used. Russians say:

2:05—пять мину́т тре́тьего (genitive of тре́тий)	five minutes of the third hour
2:55—без пяти́ три	without five: three
3:30—полови́на четвёртого (genitive of четвёртый)	half of the fourth
7:40—без двадцати́ во́семь	without twenty: eight
7:00 A.M.—семь часо́в утра́	seven o'clock in the morning
7:00 P.M.—семь часо́в ве́чера	seven o'clock in the evening
Ско́лько сейча́с вре́мени? (Кото́рый час?)	What time is it now? [Which is now the hour?]

Во ско́лько (в кото́ром часу́) **отхо́дит по́езд?**	When [at what hour] does the train leave?
Сейча́с двена́дцать часо́в дня, час дня.	It's now twelve noon, one o'clock in the afternoon.
Де́сять мину́т пя́того.	Ten minutes after four [ten minutes of the fifth (hour)].
Без че́тверти шесть.	A quarter [without a quarter] of six.
Де́сять часо́в утра́.	Ten o'clock in the morning.
Семь часо́в ве́чера.	Seven o'clock in the evening.
По́лдень.	Noon.
По́лночь.	Midnight.
Полови́на пе́рвого.	Half past twelve.
Полови́на второ́го.	Half past one.
Че́тверть тре́тьего.	A quarter after two [a quarter of the third].
Спекта́кль начина́ется без че́тверти во́семь.	The performance starts at a quarter of eight.
Э́та кни́га была́ напи́сана в ты́сяча девятьсо́т во́семьдесят пя́том году́.	This book was written in 1985 [one thousand, nine hundred, eighty-fifth year].

NOTE

After без (without), the genitive is used.

Мои́ часы́ отстаю́т.	My watch is slow.
Мои́ часы́ спеша́т.	My watch is fast.
Мои́ часы́ стоя́т.	My watch isn't running. [has stopped].

NOTE

Часы́ (watch or clock) is always used in the plural and takes a plural verb.

C. Comparative of Adjectives

To form the comparative of an adjective, drop the gender ending and add -ее for all gender endings and the plural. The adjective does not decline in the comparative:

краси́вый	pretty
краси́в-ее	prettier
тёплый	warm
тепл-е́е	warmer
весёлый	merry
весел-е́е	merrier

Irregular comparative forms:

хоро́ший	good
лу́чше	better
большо́й	big
бо́льше	bigger
ма́ленький	small
ме́ньше	smaller
широ́кий	wide
ши́ре	wider
у́зкий	narrow
у́же	narrower
плохо́й	bad
ху́же	worse
высо́кий	tall
вы́ше	taller
ти́хий	quiet

ти́ше	quieter
дорого́й	dear/expensive
доро́же	dearer/more expensive
просто́й	simple
про́ще	simpler
то́лстый	fat
то́лще	fatter

Москва́ бо́льше чем Ха́рьков.	Moscow is larger than Kharkov.
Во́лга длинне́е Днепра́.	The Volga is longer than the Dnieper.
Нью-Йорк са́мый большо́й го́род в США.	New York is the largest city in the U.S.
Здесь (о́чень) хо́лодно.	It's (very) cold here.
Сего́дня холодне́е, чем вчера́.	It's colder today than yesterday.
Вчера́ бы́ло о́чень тепло́.	It was very warm yesterday.
Зимо́й на ю́ге тепле́е, чем на се́вере.	In the winter it's warmer in the south than in the north.
Рестора́н, где мы е́ли вчера́, вообще́ лу́чше.	The restaurant where we ate yesterday is better in general.
Пойдёмте туда́.	Let's go there.

D. Superlative of Adjectives

The superlative of adjectives is formed in different ways. The simplest method, however, is to add са́мый, са́мая, са́мое, or са́мые (the most) to the adjective. For instance:

са́мый большо́й	the biggest
са́мая краси́вая	the prettiest
са́мые у́мные	the most clever

Са́мый declines with the adjective:

в са́мом большо́м до́ме	in the very largest house
Он пришёл с са́мой краси́вой же́нщиной.	He came with the prettiest woman.

QUIZ 12

1. Сего́дня холодне́е, чем вчера́.
2. Я люблю́ жить в дере́вне ле́том.
3. Я бо́льше, чем мой брат.
4. Како́й го́род са́мый большо́й в мире́?
5. Рестора́н, где мы е́ли вчера́, лу́чше.
6. Она́ всегда́ пьёт ко́фе с молоко́м.
7. Переда́йте мне, пожа́луйста, са́хар.
8. Ко́фе без молока́ гора́здо вкусне́е.
9. Ско́лько сейча́с вре́мени?
10. Когда́ (во ско́лько) вы бу́дете до́ма?
11. Де́сять мину́т пя́того.
12. Без десяти́ шесть.
13. Полови́на пе́рвого.
14. Конце́рт начина́ется без че́тверти во́семь.
15. Семь часо́в ве́чера.

a. The restaurant where we ate yesterday is better.
b. Pass [me] the sugar, please.
c. What time is it now?
d. Half-past twelve.
e. The concert starts at a quarter to eight.
f. Coffee without milk tastes much better.
g. Ten minutes to six.
h. It's colder today than yesterday.
i. Which city is the largest in the world?
j. I love to live in the country in the summer.
k. She always drinks coffee with milk.
l. Ten minutes past four.
m. Seven P.M.
n. I am bigger than my brother.
o. When (at what time) will you be home?

ANSWERS

1—h; 2—j; 3—n; 4—i; 5—a; 6—k; 7—b; 8—f; 9—c; 10—o; 11—l; 12—g; 13—d; 14—e; 15—m.

LESSON 23

A. Negatives

Я ничего́ не зна́ю.	I don't know anything.
Он ничего́ не хо́чет де́лать.	He doesn't want to do anything.
Не на́до ему́ ничего́ говори́ть.	You shouldn't tell him anything.
Мне ничего́ не на́до.	I don't need anything.
Она́ никуда́ не хо́чет идти́.	She doesn't want to go anywhere.
Они́ никогда́ не говоря́т, куда́ они́ иду́т.	They never say where they are going.
Тут о́чень темно́, я ничего́ не ви́жу.	It's very dark here; I can't see anything.
Никто́ не зна́ет, как дойти́ до библиоте́ки.	No one knows how to get to the library.
Я был в магази́не и ничего́ не купи́л.	I was at the store but didn't buy anything.
Я ещё нигде́ не был.	I haven't been anywhere yet.
Мы здесь уже́ две неде́ли и ещё не получи́ли ни одного́ письма́.	We have already been here two weeks and still haven't received one letter.

NOTE

A second (double) negative must be used with the following words:

ничего́	nothing
никто́	nobody
никогда́	never
никуда́	nowhere

Я ничего́ не зна́ю.	I don't know anything.
Никто́ не говори́т.	No one is speaking.
Мы никогда́ не бы́ли в Москве́.	We've never been to Moscow.

A negative adverb or pronoun must also use a negative with the verb it modifies. Negative words with не, on the other hand (не́чего, не́кого, не́когда, не́где, не́куда), are not used with a negated verb:

Мне не́где жить.	There's nowhere for me to live.
Мне не́когда чита́ть.	I have no time to read.
Мне не́куда идти́.	I have nowhere to go.

B. Predicative Form of Adjectives

Qualitative adjectives have two forms: the regular, which is called long, and a short form, so called because its ending is shortened. The masculine ends in a hard consonant, the feminine in -а, neuter in -о or -е, and plural in -ы or -и.

Long	Short			
	Masc.	Fem.	Neuter	Plural
ста́рый	стар	стара́	ста́ро	ста́ры

This short form is used only as a predicate:

Э́та ста́рая кни́га лежи́т на столе́.	This old book is lying on the table.
Он стар.	He is old (predicate).

C. Asking Directions

Я иностра́нец.	I'm a foreigner.
Я ничего́ не зна́ю в э́том го́роде.	I don't know anything about [in] this city.
Скажи́те, пожа́луйста, где здесь по́чта.	Please tell me where the post office is.
Два кварта́ла пря́мо, пото́м оди́н кварта́л напра́во.	Two blocks straight ahead, then one block to the right.
Большо́й дом на углу́, э́то по́чта.	The big building on the corner—that's the post office.
А что э́то за дом нале́во?	And what is this building on the left?
Э́то библиоте́ка.	That's the library.
Вы не зна́ете, где нахо́дится Большо́й теа́тр?	Do you know where the Bolshoi Theatre is?
Да, зна́ю.	Yes, I know.
Как туда́ прое́хать?	How do you get there?
Вам ну́жно сесть на тролле́йбус и прое́хать три остано́вки.	You have to take a trolleybus and go three stops.
Сойди́те на Театра́льной пло́щади, и там вы уви́дите Большо́й теа́тр.	Get off at Theatre Square, and there you'll see the Bolshoi Theatre.

А где остано́вка тролле́йбуса?	And where is the trolleybus stop?
На той стороне́ у́лицы. Вы мо́жете перейти́ на ту сто́рону то́лько на зелёный свет.	On that side of the street. You can cross to the other side only when the light is green.
Как ча́сто хо́дят тролле́йбусы?	How often do the trolleybuses run?
Ка́ждые пять мину́т.	Every five minutes.
Все тролле́йбусы на э́той остано́вке иду́т к Большо́му теа́тру?	do all trolleybuses at that stop go to the Bolshoi Theatre?
Нет. То́лько тролле́йбус но́мер де́сять. Но́мер де́вять идёт на вокза́л, а но́мер семна́дцать в аэропо́рт.	No. Only trolleybus Number 10. Number 9 goes to the train station, and Number 17 goes to the airport.
Вы не зна́ете, что сего́дня идёт в Большо́м теа́тре?	And do [would] you know what is playing today at the Bolshoi Theatre?
Как же! Коне́чно зна́ю! Идёт «Лебеди́ное о́зеро».	What a question! Of course I do! *Swan Lake* is playing.
Что вы говори́те! Я давно́ хочу́ посмотре́ть э́тот бале́т.	You don't say! I've wanted to see that ballet for a long time.
Большо́е спаси́бо.	Thanks a lot.
О́чень вам благода́рен.	I'm very grateful to you.
Пожа́луйста.	You're welcome.

QUIZ 13

1. Он ничего́ не зна́ет.
2. Она́ ничего́ не хо́чет.
3. Мы никого́ не лю́бим.
4. Я не получи́л ни одного́ письма́.
5. Что э́то за кни́га?
6. Он давно́ хо́чет посмотре́ть э́тот ба́лет.
7. Я иностра́нец. Я ничего́ не зна́ю в э́том го́роде.
8. Она́ ещё нигде́ не была́.
9. Скажи́те, пожа́луйста, где здесь по́чта?
10. Они́ никогда́ не говоря́т, куда́ они́ иду́т.
11. Я не зна́ю, где они́ бы́ли вчера́.
12. Что сего́дня идёт в теа́тре?
13. Я не зна́ю. Я никогда́ ничего́ не зна́ю.
14. Большо́е спаси́бо.
15. Вам ну́жно прое́хать три остано́вки.

a. I don't know where they were yesterday
b. I don't know. I never know anything.
c. She hasn't been anywhere yet.
d. I am a foreigner. I know nothing about [in] this town.
e. Thanks a lot.
f. Tell me, please, where the post office is.
g. I haven't received one letter.
h. She doesn't want anything.
i. What's playing at the theatre today?
j. He has wanted to see this ballet for a long time.
k. We don't love anyone.
l. What sort of book is this?
m. He doesn't know anything.
n. You have to go three stops.
o. They never say where they are going.

ANSWERS

1—m; 2—h; 3—k; 4—g; 5—l; 6—j; 7—d; 8—c; 9—f; 10—o; 11—a; 12—i; 13—b; 14—e; 15—n.

LESSON 24

A. Sample Sentences: Small Talk

Вчера́ бы́ло воскресе́нье.	Yesterday was Sunday.
Вчера́ никто́ не рабо́тал.	Yesterday no one was working.
Мы сиде́ли до́ма весь день.	We stayed home all day.
Ле́том на да́че бы́ло о́чень жа́рко.	It was very hot in the country during the summer.
Я был на ле́кции.	I was at the lecture.
Ле́ктор говори́л об Аме́рике.	The lecturer was talking about America.
Он сказа́л, что в Ю́жной Аме́рике говоря́т по-испа́нски и по-португа́льски.	He said that in South America they speak Spanish and Portuguese.
Я учи́л англи́йский язы́к, когда́ я был ещё ма́леньким ма́льчиком.	I studied English when I was still a small boy.
Толсто́й написа́л рома́н «Война́ и мир».	Tolstoi wrote the novel *War and Peace*.
Его́ жена́ ему́ всегда́ помога́ла.	His wife was always helping him.
Он мог рабо́тать по це́лым дням.	He could work for days at a time.
Она́ могла́ писа́ть мно́го часо́в в день.	She could write many hours a day.
Говоря́т, что она́ переписывала э́тот рома́н де́сять раз.	They say that she copied this novel ten times.

Я уста́л.	I was tired.
Я устаю́, когда́ (я) **мно́го говорю́.**	I become tired when I talk a lot.
Он устава́л о́чень бы́стро.	He used to become tired very quickly.
Она́ опозда́ла.	She was late.
Она́ всегда́ опа́здывает.	She is always late.
Они́ шли домо́й, когда́ неожи́данно пошёл дождь.	They were walking home when it started to rain unexpectedly.
Дождь шёл це́лый день (весь день), **всю неде́лю, весь ме́сяц.**	It rained [rain fell] all day, all week, all month.
Секрета́рша пришла́ на рабо́ту и начала́ печа́тать.	The secretary arrived at work and began to type.
Он игра́л. Она́ слу́шала. Он ко́нчил игра́ть.	He played. She listened. He finished playing.
Она́ заговори́ла.	She began to speak.
В час дня все пошли́ обе́дать.	At one o'clock everyone went to have lunch.
Я пообе́дала и верну́лась на рабо́ту.	I had lunch [lunched] and returned to work.
Он был здесь не́сколько дней тому́ наза́д.	He was here several days ago.
Я прие́хала в Москву́ две неде́ли тому́ наза́д.	I came to Moscow two weeks ago.
Я ещё не получи́ла ни одного́ письма́.	I still haven't received a single letter.

По́чта прихо́дит ра́но у́тром.	The mail comes early in the morning.
Она́ ду́мала, что здесь все говоря́т по-англи́йски.	She thought that everyone spoke English here.
Она́ купи́ла всё, что ей бы́ло ну́жно.	She bought everything [all] that she needed.
Он купи́л мно́го нену́жных вещёй.	He bought a lot of unnecessary things.
Она́ люби́ла его́ когда́-то.	She loved him at one time.
И он люби́л её, но э́то бы́ло мно́го лет тому́ наза́д.	And he loved her too, but that was many years ago.

B. Verbs: Perfective and Imperfective Aspects

Russian verbs can be perfective or imperfective. Imperfective verbs express continuous or repeated action. They have three tenses: past, present, and future.

Perfective verbs indicate completion of action, beginning of action, or both, and have only two tenses: past and future.

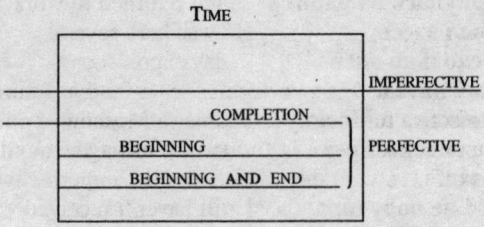

Some perfective verbs are formed by adding prefixes—such as с, на, вы, в, по—to imperfective verbs. When a prefix is added to a verb, very often the meaning of the verb is changed at the same time.

IMPERFECTIVE	PERFECTIVE
писа́ть to write	написа́ть to write down to finish writing
	переписать to copy

When the meaning of the verb changes, the new verb (переписа́ть, to copy) that has been formed must have its own imperfective. To form the imperfective of such new verbs, the suffix -ыв, -ив or -ав is added:

IMPERFECTIVE	PERFECTIVE	IMPERFECTIVE
писа́ть (to write)	переписа́ть (to copy)	перепи́сывать
чита́ть (to read)	прочита́ть (to finish reading or to read through)	прочи́тывать
	перечита́ть (to read over)	перечи́тывать
знать (to know)	узна́ть (to find out or to recognize)	узнава́ть

The past tense of the perfective is formed in the same manner as the past tense of the imperfective.

C. THE FUTURE TENSE

The future tense has two forms: imperfective future and perfective future. As has already been pointed out, the imperfective future is formed by using the auxiliary verb быть with the infinitive of the imperfective verb.

я бу́ду	I will
ты бу́дешь	you will
он бу́дет говори́ть, чита́ть	he will speak, read,
мы бу́дем понима́ть, etc.	we will understand, etc.
вы бу́дете	you will
они́ бу́дут	they will

The perfective future is formed without using the auxiliary verb быть.

PRESENT		PERFECTIVE FUTURE	
я пишу́	I write	я напишу́	I will write
ты говори́шь	you speak	ты ска́жешь	you will say
он идёт	he goes	он придёт	he will come
мы чита́ем	we read	мы прочита́ем	we will read
вы смо́трите	you look	вы посмо́трите	you will look
они́ е́дут	they go [ride]	они́ прие́дут	they will come [ride]

NOTE

The perfective verb is conjugated in the future in the same way that the imperfective is conjugated in the present.

QUIZ 14

1. Ле́ктор говори́л об Аме́рике.
2. Вчера́ я писа́л весь день.
3. Она́ написа́ла вчера́ два письма́.
4. Он сказа́л, что он ничего́ не зна́ет.
5. Она́ всегда́ э́то говори́т.
6. Она́ опозда́ла сего́дня.
7. Дождь шёл це́лый день.

a. He was in town.
b. I had breakfast and returned to work.
c. She always says that.
d. At one o'clock everyone went to lunch.
e. She was home.
f. She is always late.
g. Yesterday I wrote all day.

8. Она́ всегда́ опа́здывает.
9. В час дня все пошли́ обе́дать.
10. Он купи́л мно́го нену́жных веще́й.
11. Я поза́втракал и верну́лся на рабо́ту.
12. Она́ была́ до́ма.
13. Он был в го́роде.
14. Мы бы́ли на рабо́те.
15. Он был в Аме́рике мно́го лет тому́ наза́д.

h. She was late today.
i. He was in America many years ago.
j. He said that he knows nothing.
k. We were at work.
l. The lecturer was talking about America.
m. She wrote two letters yesterday.
n. It was raining all day.
o. He bought a lot of unnecessary things.

ANSWERS

1—l; 2—g; 3—m; 4—j; 5—c; 6—h; 7—n; 8—f; 9—d; 10—o; 11—b; 12—e; 13—a; 14—k; 15—i.

LESSON 25

A. Meeting a Friend in Moscow

Здра́вствуйте, Никола́й Ива́нович!	Hello, Nikolai Ivanovich.
Здравствуйте, Наде́жда Петро́вна, как давно́ я вас не ви́дел!	Hello, Nadezhda Petrovna, I haven't seen you in a long time.
Вы давно́ в Москве́?	Have you been in Moscow long?
Нет. Я прие́хал неде́лю тому́ наза́д.	No. I arrived a week ago.
Где вы живёте?	Where are you staying [living]?
Я живу́ у бра́та. У него́ больша́я кварти́ра.	I'm staying [living] with my brother. He has a large apartment.
Ваш брат хорошо́ говори́т по-англи́йски, пра́вда?	Your brother speaks English well, doesn't he? [isn't it true?]
Да. Он говори́т, пи́шет и чита́ет по-англи́йски.	Yes. He speaks, writes, and reads English.
Его́ жена́ америка́нка, да?	His wife is an American, isn't she?
Да, вот почему́ он так хорошо́ зна́ет англи́йский язы́к.	Yes, that's why he knows English so well.
Скажи́те, а как его́ жена́ говори́т по-ру́сски?	Tell me, how well does his wife speak Russian?
Не о́чень хорошо́.	Not very well.
Она́ понима́ет почти́	She understands almost

всё, но говори́т пло́хо.	everything, but speaks poorly.
Вы давно́ зна́ете его́ жену́?	Have you known his wife for a long time?
Коне́чно. Я знал её ра́ньше моего́ бра́та.	Of course. I knew her before my brother did.
Говоря́т, что она́ о́чень ми́лая же́нщина.	They say that she's a very pleasant woman.
Да, она́ у́мная, краси́вая и о́чень ми́лая.	Yes, she's intelligent, pretty, and very pleasant.
У них есть де́ти?	Do they have children?
Да, есть.	Yes, they do.
А как они́ говоря́т– по-ру́сски и́ли по-англи́йски?	What do they speak— Russian or English?
Де́ти говоря́т и по-ру́сски и по-англи́йски.	The children speak both Russian and English.
Как э́то хорошо́! Я ду́маю, что все де́ти должны́ знать хотя́ бы два языка́	Isn't that good! I think that all children should know at least two languages.
Ну, коне́чно, все должны́ знать два языка́.	Well, of course everybody should know two languages.
Вот вы–ру́сский и о́чень хорошо́ говори́те. по-англи́йски.	Well, you're Russian, and you speak English very well.
А вы–америка́нка и о́чень хорошо́ говори́те по-ру́сски.	And you're an American and speak Russian very well.
Нет, ещё не о́чень хорошо́, но я всё	No, not very well yet, but I'm studying all

вре́мя занима́юсь и бу́ду хорошо́ говори́ть по-ру́сски.	the time and will speak Russian well.
С кем вы занима́етесь?	With whom are you studying?
Ра́ньше у меня́ был о́чень хоро́ший учи́тель, но он уе́хал, потому́ что его́ мать заболе́ла. И тепе́рь я занима́юсь сама́.	I had a very good teacher before, but he went away because his mother became ill. And now I'm studying by myself.
Но вы зна́ете, э́то о́чень тру́дно.	But you know, that's very difficult.
Коне́чно, тру́дно занима́ться само́й, но я уже доста́точно мно́го прошла́, а чем бо́льше вы зна́ете, тем ле́гче продолжа́ть.	Of course it's difficult to study by oneself, but I've already gone through quite a lot, and the more you know, the easier it is to continue.

B. The Personal Pronouns: Сам, Себя́

The personal pronoun сам, сама́, само́, са́ми (by oneself) is declined like other personal pronouns (see table, Lesson 11). It can modify the subject of the sentence, emphasizing that the action is performed independently, or a complement, with the meaning that it is a specific complement and not any other.

The reflexive pronoun себя́ (oneself) has no gender and no nominative form. It refers back to the subject.

Я занима́юсь сам.	I study by myself.
Я сказа́л ему́ самому́.	I told him [himself].
Само́ собо́й. разуме́ется.	It goes without saying. [It reasons itself.]
Он разгова́ривает сам с собо́й.	He talks to himself. [himself with himself].
Он никогда́ сам о себе́ ничего́ не говори́т.	He never says anything about himself.
Она́ взяла́ с собо́й мою́ кни́гу.	She took my book with her.
Она́ сама́ сши́ла себе́ пла́тье.	She made a dress for herself.

The verb жить (to live), although it ends in -ить, belongs to the first conjunction and is conjugated as follows:

я живу́	I live
ты живёшь	you live
он живёт	he lives
мы живём	we live
вы живёте	you live
они живу́т	they live

C. Word Study

стро́ить-постро́ить	to build
внима́тельно	attentively
конча́ть-ко́нчить	to finish
па́мятник	monument
нау́чный	scholarly
обсужда́ть-обсуди́ть	to discuss
ме́сяц	month
всегда́	always
пока́	so long

QUIZ 15

1. Она́ ру́сская и о́чень хорошо́ говори́т по-англи́йски.
2. Где вы живёте?
3. Скажи́те, как его́ жена́ говори́т по-ру́сски?
4. У них есть де́ти.
5. Вы давно́ зна́ете его́?
6. Ра́ньше у меня́ был о́чень хоро́ший учи́тель.
7. Я всё вре́мя занима́юсь.
8. Мы бу́дем хорошо́ говори́ть по-русски.
9. Они́ прие́хали в Москву́ неде́лю тому́ наза́д.
10. Я занима́юсь сам.
11. Чем бо́льше вы зна́ете, тем ле́гче продолжа́ть.
12. Он уе́хал, потому́ что его́ мать заболе́ла.
13. Все должны́ знать хотя́ бы два языка́.
14. С кем вы занима́етесь?
15. Я давно́ вас не ви́дел.

a. I study all the time.
b. They have children.
c. The more you know, the easier it is to continue.
d. I haven't seen you in a long time.
e. We will speak Russian well.
f. With whom are you studying?
g. She is Russian and speaks English very well.
h. He went away because his mother became ill.
i. Where do you live?
j. Have you known him long?
k. Tell me, how well does his wife speak Russian?
l. I had a very good teacher before.
m. They arrived in Moscow a week ago.
n. Everyone should know at least two languages.
o. I study by myself.

ANSWERS

1—g; 2—i; 3—k; 4—b; 5—j; 6—l; 7—a; 8—e; 9—m; 10—o; 11—c; 12—h; 13—n; 14—f; 15—d.

LESSON 26

A. Shopping: In a Store

Где здесь хоро́ший магази́н?	Where is there a good store here?

Како́й магази́н вам ну́жен?	What kind of a store do you need?
Мне ну́жно купи́ть бума́гу, каранда́ши́ и словари́.	I have to buy paper, pencils, and dictionaries.
Есть тако́й магази́н на Не́вском проспе́кте.	There's a store like that on Nevsky Prospect.
(В магази́не)	(In the store)
У вас есть словари́?	Do you have dictionaries?
Коне́чно. Како́й слова́рь вам ну́жен?	Of course. What kind of dictionary do you need?
Я америка́нец, и как вы слы́шите, не совсе́м хорошо́ говорю́ по-ру́сски.	I'm an American, and, as you (can) hear, I don't speak Russian too well.
Очеви́дно, вам нужны́ ру́сско-англи́йский и а́нгло-ру́сский словари́. Вот о́ба словаря́ в одно́м то́ме, а вот побо́льше, в двух тома́х.	Obviously you need Russian-English and English-Russian dictionaries. Here are both dictionaries in one volume, and this one a bit larger, in two volumes.
Ско́лько они́ сто́ят?	How much do they cost?
Одното́мный пятьсо́т во́семьдесят рубле́й, а двухто́мный ты́сяча сто шестьдеся́т.	The one-volume [dictionary] five hundred eighty rubles, and the two-volume, one thousand one hundred sixty.
Как вы ду́маете, како́й из них лу́чше? Я не зна́ю.	What do you think—which of them is better? I don't know.

Э́то де́ло вку́са.	It's a question of taste.
Е́сли вы мно́го чита́ете и перево́дите, возьми́те большо́й.	If you read a lot and translate, take the big one.
Нет, мне ну́жен слова́рь то́лько для разгово́ра.	No, I need a dictionary only for conversation.
Ну, тогда́ возьми́те ма́ленький. Его́ удо́бно носи́ть с собо́й.	Well, then, take the little one. It's convenient to carry with you.
Скажи́те, пожа́луйста, а у вас есть карандаши́?	Tell me, please, do you have pencils?
Вот чёрные карандаши́, вот кра́сные и си́ние.	Here are black pencils; here are red and blue ones.
Э́ти твёрдые, а э́ти мя́гкие.	These are hard, and these are soft.
Покажи́те мне, пожа́луйста, автору́чки.	Please show me (some) fountain pens.
Вот э́то о́чень хоро́шая ру́чка. Мы гаранти́руем, что она́ не бу́дет течь.	Here's a very good pen. We guarantee that it won't leak.
Ну, вот и хорошо́. Э́то, пожа́луй, всё.	That's good. I think that's all.
Да́йте мне двена́дцать карандаше́й, одну́ ру́чку и вот э́ту коро́бку пи́счей бума́ги.	Give me a dozen pencils, one pen, and that box of writing paper there.
А слова́рь вы не возьмёте?	Aren't you going to take the dictionary?

Ах да! Коне́чно! Да́йте мне ма́ленький, одното́мный.	Oh yes! Of course! Give me the little one-volume (dictionary).
Ско́лько с меня́?	How much do I owe you?
Слова́рь пятьсо́т во́семьдесят рубле́й, каранда́ши три́ддцать рубле́й, ру́чка сто де́сять рубле́й и бума́га се́мьдесят рубле́й—все́го семьсо́т девяно́сто рубле́й.	The dictionary is five hundred eighty rubles; the pencils, thirty rubles; the pen, one hundred and ten rubles; and the paper, seventy rubles—in all, seven hundred and ninety rubles.
Пожа́луйста.	Here you are.
Спаси́бо. Всего́ хоро́шего.	Thank you. All the best.
До свида́ния.	Good-bye.
Заходи́те ещё.	Come again!

B. Perfective Verbs with Different Roots

Imperfective	Perfective	Imperfective
говори́ть (to speak)	сказа́ть (to tell)	
	заговори́ть (to begin talking)	загова́ривать
	рассказа́ть (to tell a story)	расска́зывать
	заказа́ть (to order something to be made or done)	зака́зывать
	приказа́ть (to order, to command)	прика́зывать

Prefixes can be added to either говори́ть or каза́ть, but each combination forms a new verb; e.g.:

за-говори́ть	to begin talking
за-каза́ть	to order something
от-говори́ть	to talk someone out of something
от-каза́ть	to refuse

The perfective of the verb брать (*to take*) is взять. They are conjugated as follows:

Present Tense		Perfective Future	
брать		взять	
я беру́	I take	я возьму́	I will take
ты берёшь	you take	ты возьмёшь	you will take
он берёт	he takes	он возьмёт	he will take
мы берём	we take	мы возьмём	we will take
вы берёте	you take	вы возьмёте	you will take
они беру́т	they take	они возьму́т	they will take

QUIZ 16

1. Вот о́ба словаря́ в одно́м то́ме.
2. Как вы ду́маете, како́й из них лу́чше?
3. Покажи́те мне, пожа́луйста, автору́чки.
4. Да́йте мне двена́дцать карандаше́й.
5. Как вы слы́шите, я не совсе́м хорошо́ говорю́ по-ру́сски.
6. Мне ну́жен слова́рь то́лько для разгово́ра.
7. Я специа́льно за э́тим пришёл.
8. Ско́лько они́ сто́ят?

a. These pencils are hard, and these are soft.
b. I need a dictionary only for conversation.
c. In all, one hundred seventy-six thousand rubles.
d. I came especially for that.
e. If you read and translate a lot, take the big one.
f. I need a bookstore.
g. Here are both dictionaries in one volume.
h. Give me twelve pencils.

9. Всего́ сто се́мьдесят шесть ты́сяч рубле́й.
10. Очеви́дно, вам ну́жен большо́й хоро́ший слова́рь.
11. Е́сли вы мно́го чита́ете и перево́дите, возьми́те большо́й.
12. Э́ти каранда́ши твёрдые, а э́ти мя́гкие.
13. Мне ну́жен кни́жный магази́н.
14. Какой слова́рь вам ну́жен?
15. Всего́ хоро́шего. Заходи́те ещё.

i. Please show me (some) fountain pens.
j. What do you think—which of them is better?
k. How much do they cost?
l. All the best. Come again.
m. What kind of a dictionary do you need?
n. As you (can) hear, I don't speak Russian well.
o. Obviously you need a good, big dictionary.

ANSWERS
1—g; 2—j; 3—i; 4—h; 5—n; 6—b; 7—d; 8—k; 9—c; 10—o; 11—e; 12—a; 13—f; 14—m; 15—l.

LESSON 27

A. Verbs of Motion

Verbs of motion have many variations of meaning. A different verb is used to express movement by a conveyance than is used to express movement by foot.

Each of these verbs has two forms: i.e., one describes a single action in one direction; the other, a repeated action. All of these forms are imperfective. The perfective is formed by adding a prefix to a single-action verb. However, it must be emphasized that the addition of the prefix changes the meaning of the verb. The same prefix with the repeated-action verb forms the imperfective of the new verb.

Study the following chart.

IMPERFECTIVE	REPEATED ACTION		ONE ACTION	PERFECTIVE
	ходи́ть	to go on foot	идти́	
	е́здить	to go by vehicle	е́хать	
выходи́ть		to go out on foot		вы́йти
выезжа́ть		to go out by vehicle		вы́ехать
приходи́ть		to come on foot [arrive]		прийти́
приезжа́ть		to come by vehicle [arrive]		прие́хать
заходи́ть		to drop in [visit] on foot		зайти́
заезжа́ть		to drop in [visit] by vehicle		зае́хать
	носи́ть	to carry on foot	нести́	
	вози́ть	to carry by vehicle	везти́	
приноси́ть		to bring on foot		принести́
привози́ть		to bring by vehicle		привезти́

ИДТИ́ TO GO ON FOOT (SINGLE ACTION IN ONE DIRECTION)	
PRESENT TENSE	PAST TENSE
я иду́ ты идёшь он идёт мы идём вы идёте они́ иду́т	он шёл она́ шла оно́ шло они́ шли

ХОДИ́ТЬ TO GO ON FOOT (REPEATED ACTION)	
PRESENT TENSE	PAST TENSE
я хожу́ ты хо́дишь он хо́дит мы хо́дим вы хо́дите они́ хо́дят	Regular

É́ХАТЬ TO GO BY VEHICLE (SINGLE ACTION IN ONE DIRECTION)	
PRESENT TENSE	PAST TENSE
я е́ду ты е́дешь он е́дет мы е́дем вы е́дете они́ е́дут	Regular

éздить TO GO BY VEHICLE (REPEATED ACTION)	
PRESENT TENSE	PAST TENSE
я éзжу ты éздишь он éздит мы éздим вы éздите они́ éздят	Regular

нести́ TO CARRY ON FOOT (SINGLE ACTION IN ONE DIRECTION)	
PRESENT TENSE	PAST TENSE
я несу́ ты несёшь он несёт мы несём вы несёте они́ несу́т	 он нёс она́ несла́ оно́ несло́ они́ несли́

носи́ть TO CARRY ON FOOT (REPEATED ACTION)	
PRESENT TENSE	PAST TENSE
я ношу́ ты но́сишь он но́сит мы но́сим вы но́сите они́ но́сят	Regular

везти́ TO CARRY BY VEHICLE (SINGLE ACTION IN ONE DIRECTION)	
PRESENT TENSE	PAST TENSE
я везу́ ты везёшь он везёт вы везём вы везёте они́ везу́т	он вёз она́ везла́ оно́ везло́ они́ везли́

вози́ть TO CARRY BY VEHICLE (REPEATED ACTION)	
PRESENT TENSE	PAST TENSE
я вожу́ ты во́зишь он во́зит мы во́зим вы во́зите они́ во́зят	Regular

QUIZ 17

In this quiz, or exercise, try to fill in the blanks with the proper form of "going" verbs, on foot or by vehicle, in one direction or denoting repeated action. Think carefully before choosing your answers.

1. Мы _____ сего́дня из Чика́го в Нью-Йорк.	Today we came to New York from Chicago.
2. Я _____ в библиоте́ку ка́ждый деиь.	I go to the library every day.
3. Сего́дня он не _____ в библиоте́ку.	Today he is not going to the library.
4. Они́ _____ на да́чу ка́ждый год.	They go to the country every year.
5. В э́том году́ они́ _____ к мо́рю.	This year they are going to the seashore.
6. Я ви́дел её сего́дня, когда́ она́ _____ в шко́лу.	I saw her today when she was going to school.
7. Она́ _____ с собо́й две кни́ги.	She was carrying two books with her.
8. Наша́ шко́ла о́чень далеко́ и мы должны́ _____ на авто́бусе.	Our school is very far, and we have to [must] go by bus.

ANSWERS

1. прие́хали; 2. хожу́; 3. идёт; 4. е́здят; 5. е́дут; 6. шла; 7. несла́; 8. е́здить.

B. In a Hotel

Здра́вствуйте. Мы то́лько что прие́хали из Нью-Йо́рка.	Hello. We've just arrived from New York.
У вас есть свобо́дные номера́?	Do you have any vacant [free] rooms?
Да, есть.	Yes, we do (have).
На како́м этаже́ э́ти номера́?	What floor are these rooms on?
На пя́том.	On the fifth.

Э́тот номер сли́шком тёмный.	This room is too dark.
На девя́том этаже́ есть но́мер, о́кна кото́рого выхо́дят на у́лицу.	On the ninth floor there is a room where the windows [the windows of which] face the street.
Мо́жно посмотре́ть?	May I see it? [Is it possible to look?]
Да, пожа́луйста.	Yes, please.
Э́тот но́мер мне о́чень нра́вится.	I like this room very much.
Пожа́луйста, принеси́те мо́й бага́ж (мои́ ве́щи) **сюда́.**	Please bring my baggage [my things] here.
Скажи́те, пожа́луйста, есть ли здесь парикма́херская?	Tell me, please, is there a barbershop here?
Парикма́херская–на второ́м этаже́.	The barbershop is on the second floor.
Она́ откры́та с девяти́ часо́в утра́ до пяти́ часо́в ве́чера.	It's open from nine in the morning to five o'clock in the afternoon.
А на како́м этаже́ портно́й?	And what floor is the tailor on?
Мне на́до погла́дить костю́м.	I have to have a suit pressed.
Портно́й на пя́том этаже́.	The tailor is on the fifth floor.
Кому́ мо́жно отда́ть бельё?	To whom should [may] I give my laundry?
Тут у меня́ не́сколько руба́шек и ни́жнее бельё.	I have [here] several shirts and some underwear.

Вы мо́жете отда́ть ва́ше бельё де́вушке, кото́рая убира́ет ва́шу ко́мнату.	You may turn in your laundry to the girl who cleans your room.
Когда́ оно́ бу́дет гото́во?	When will it be ready?
Бельё обы́чно гото́во че́рез два дня.	Laundry is usually ready in two days.
Э́то меня́ вполне́ устра́ивает.	That suits me completely.
А мо́жно заказа́ть за́втрак к себе́ в но́мер?	May I order breakfast in my room?
Коне́чно. На ка́ждом этаже́ есть своё обслу́живание.	Of course. Each floor has its own service.

C. Imperfective and Perfective Forms of "To Give"

Imperfective (present)		Perfective (future)	
дава́ть		дать	
я даю́	I give	я дам	I will give
ты даёшь	you give	ты дашь	you will give
он даёт	he gives	он даст	he will give
мы даём	we give	мы дади́м	we will give
вы даёте	you give	вы дади́те	you will give
они́ даю́т	they give	они́ даду́т	they will give

от-дава́ть	to give out, away	от-да́ть
пере-дава́ть	to pass	пере-да́ть
за-дава́ть	to assign	за-да́ть
с-дава́ть	to deal (cards)	с-дать

D. In My Apartment

В ко́мнате стои́т стол и два сту́ла. На одно́й стене́ вис́ит ка́рта го́рода, а на друго́й две карти́ны. До́ма у меня́ в кварти́ре две ко́мнаты: спа́льня и гости́ная. Гости́ная о́чень больша́я. В гости́ной три окна́ и все выхо́дят на у́лицу. В спа́льне то́лько одно́ окно́, и не на у́лицу. Поэ́тому в спа́льне о́чень ти́хо. В спа́льне стои́т больша́я крова́ть, комо́д и шкаф для оде́жды.

There are a table and two chairs in the room. A map of the city hangs on one wall, and two pictures on the other. I have a one-bedroom apartment [at home I have two rooms in my apartment]: a bedroom, and a living room. The living room is very big. In the living room there are three windows, all of which face the street. There is only one window in the bedroom, and that does not face the street. Therefore, the bedroom is very quiet. In the bedroom there is a large bed, a dresser, and a wardrobe.

Ку́хня ма́ленькая, но о́чень удо́бная. В ней всё есть: и га́зовая плита́, и холоди́льник, и мно́го по́лок и я́щиков для посу́ды. На окне́ в ку́хне краси́вые ро́зовые занаве́ски.

The kitchen is small, but very comfortable. It is fully equipped with [there is all (the equipment)] a gas stove, a refrigerator, and a lot of shelves and drawers for dishes. There are pretty pink curtains in the kitchen window.

QUIZ 18

1. *У* вас есть свобо́дные номера́?
2. Вы мо́жете отда́ть ва́ше бельё сего́дня и оно́ бу́дет гото́во за́втра.
3. Э́то меня́ вполне́ устра́ивает.
4. О́кна э́той ко́мнаты выхо́дят на у́лицу.
5. Скажи́те, пожа́луйста, где парикма́херская?
6. Парикма́херская–на второ́м этаже́.
7. Мы то́лько что прие́хали из Нью-Йо́рка.
8. Мне на́до погла́дить костю́м.
9. Портно́й на пя́том этаже́.
10. Конто́ра откры́та с девяти́ часо́в утра́ до пяти́ часо́в ве́чера.

a. The barbershop is on the second floor.
b. Tell me, please, where the barbershop is.
c. I have to have a suit pressed.
d. We've just arrived from New York.
e. The office is open from nine in the morning to five in the afternoon.
f. The tailor is on the fifth floor.
g. The windows of this room face the street.
h. Do you have any vacant [free] rooms?
i. This suits me completely.
j. You may turn in your laundry today, and it will be ready tomorrow.

ANSWERS
1—h; 2—j; 3—i; 4—g; 5—b; 6—a; 7—d; 8—c; 9—f; 10—e.

LESSON 28

A. In a Restaurant

Макси́м:
Вот, здесь о́коло окна́ хоро́ший сто́лик.

Maxim:
Look, here's a good table near the window.

Пётр:
О́чень хорошо́. Я о́чень люблю́ смотре́ть в окно́.

Peter:
Very good. I like to look out the window.

Макси́м:
Дава́йте посмо́трим, что сего́дня на обе́д. Бара́нина жа́реная, бифште́кс натура́льный и́ли бифште́кс ру́бленый. Бли́нчики с мя́сом. Суп из све́жих овоще́й. Карто́фельное пюре́.

Maxim:
Let's see what they have for dinner today. Lamb chops, regular steak or chopped sirloin. Blinchiki with meat. Fresh vegetable soup. Mashed potatoes.

Пётр:
Зна́ете, что я возьму́? Я хочу́ хоро́шей ры́бы. Я о́чень люблю́ ры́бу, и говоря́т, что здесь её великоле́пно гото́вят. На сла́дкое я возьму́ компо́т из сухофру́ктов.

Peter:
You know what I'll have? I want some good fish. I love fish, and they say that they prepare it very well here. For dessert I'll have a compote of dried fruit.

Макси́м:
А я съем мясны́е котле́ты и кисе́ль на сла́дкое.

Maxim:
And I'll have meat cutlets, and kissel for dessert.

Пётр:
Официа́нт! Пожа́луйста принеси́те нам буты́лочку вина́. Како́го-нибу́дь хоро́шего кавка́зского.

Peter:
Waiter! Please bring us a bottle of wine. Some good wine from the Caucasus.

Макси́м:
Ах, како́е замеча́тельное вино́. Ну, за ва́ше здоро́вье, мой дорого́й друг!

Maxim:
Ah! What excellent wine. Well, to your health, my dear friend!

Пётр:
И за ва́ше то́же!
Тепе́рь ну́жно закуси́ть. Вот кусо́чек селёдки.
Е́шьте, пожа́луйста.
Ах, как вку́сно!

Макси́м:
Ну, ещё по бока́лу.
За мир, и сча́стье всех люде́й во всём ми́ре.

Пётр:
Ну, зна́ете, за тако́й тост нельзя́ не вы́пить.

Макси́м:
Ну, ещё оди́н бока́л?

Пётр:
Нет, спаси́бо, я бо́льше не хочу́.

Макси́м:
Ну, ещё по бока́лу.

Пётр:
Нет, я сказа́л уже́, что бо́льше не хочу́, и бо́льше не бу́ду.
Дава́йте есть.

Макси́м:
Ну, ничего́ с ва́ми не поде́лаешь.
Дава́йте есть. А я вы́пил бы ещё.

Peter:
And to yours also!
Now we must eat a bit. Here's a piece of herring. Please have some. Oh, how delicious!

Maxim:
Let's each have another glass. To peace, and to the happiness of all people in the whole world.

Peter:
Well, you know, it's impossible not to drink to such a toast.

Maxim:
Well, another glass?

Peter:
No, thank you, I don't want any more.

Maxim:
Just one more!

Peter:
No, I already said that I don't want any more and won't drink any more. Let's eat.

Maxim:
Well, if I can't do anything [nothing can be done] with you . . . Let's eat. But I would

Пётр:
Вы пе́йте, а я бо́льше не хочу́.
Макси́м:
Официа́нт! Ско́лько мы вам должны́?

have had another [drunk another].
Peter:
You drink, but I don't want any more.
Maxim:
Waiter! How much do we owe you?

B. Food and Utensils

ма́сло	butter
хлеб	bread
соль	salt
пе́рец	pepper
сала́т	salad, lettuce
подли́вка	sauce, gravy
зе́лень	green vegetables
о́вощи	vegetables
стака́н воды́	glass of water
чай	tea
ко́фе	coffee
фру́кты	fruit
холо́дная заку́ска	hors d'oeuvres
второ́е блю́до	main course
сла́дкое	sweet course
десе́рт	dessert
нож	knife
столо́вая ло́жка	tablespoon or soup spoon
ча́йная ло́жечка	teaspoon
таре́лка	plate
таре́лочка	small plate
глубо́кая таре́лка	soup bowl
блю́до	platter

ча́шка	cup
блю́дце	saucer
стака́н	glass
салфе́тка	napkin
соло́нка	salt shaker

C. More: Use of Ещё or Бо́льше

The word "more" can be expressed in Russian by either ещё or бо́льше.

Вы хоти́те ещё ча́ю?	Do you want some more tea?
Нет, я бо́льше не хочу.	No, I don't want any more.
Да, я хочу́ ещё.	Yes, I want (some) more.
Я приду́ к вам ещё раз.	I will come to you once more.
Я бо́льше к вам не бу́ду приходи́ть.	I will not come to you any more.

It is generally true that to express "more" affirmatively, ещё is used; to say "no more" or "I don't want more," or when "more" is coupled with any negative verb, бо́льше is used.

Я хочу́ ещё.	I want more.
Он бо́льше не хо́чет.	He doesn't want more.
Я хочу́ ещё чита́ть.	I want to read some more.
Она́ вас бо́льше не лю́бит.	She doesn't love you any more.

D. Conjugation of "To Eat"

ЕСТЬ	TO EAT
я ем	I eat
ты ешь	you eat
он ест	he eats
мы еди́м	we eat
вы еди́те	you eat
они едя́т	they eat
Past Tense	
он ел	he
она́ е́ла	she ate
оно́ е́ло	it ate
они́ е́ли	they ate

QUIZ 19

1. Пожа́луйста, принеси́те буты́лочку вина́.
2. Нет, я бо́льше не хочу́.
3. Нет, я ещё не ко́нчил.
4. Я о́чень люблю́ ры́бу.
5. Я ещё не ел ры́бы в э́том году́.
6. Он бо́льше не хо́чет мя́са.
7. Почему́ вы бо́льше не хоти́те?
8. Потому́ что я бо́льше не го́лоден.
9. Я не ем, потому́ что я ещё не го́лоден.
10. На сла́дкое я возьму́ компо́т из сухофру́ктов.
11. Компо́та бо́льше нет.

a. I can't eat any [thing] more.
b. He doesn't want any more meat.
c. Because I am not hungry anymore.
d. There is no more compote.
e. Do you want anything else?
f. No, I don't want any more.
g. Please bring a bottle of wine.
h. I like fish very much.
i. I haven't eaten fish yet this year.
j. No, thanks, I am finished.
k. No, I haven't finished yet.

12. Вы хоти́те ещё что́-нибудь?
13. Нет, спаси́бо, я уже́ ко́нчил.
14. Я бо́льше ничего́ не могу́ съесть.
15. Жаль. А я бы вы́пил ещё.

l. Too bad. As for me, I would have had another.
m. For dessert I'll have compote of dried fruit.
n. Why don't you want any more?
o. I'm not eating because I'm not hungry yet.

ANSWERS
1—g; 2—f; 3—k; 4—h; 5—i; 6—b; 7—n; 8—c; 9—o; 10—m; 11—d; 12—e; 13—j; 14—a; 15—l.

LESSON 29

A. More on Perfective and Imperfective Verbs

This lesson provides further examples of the use of perfective and imperfective verbs.

Мы бу́дем писа́ть пи́сьма. писа́ть
We will write letters.

Я напишу́ письмо́. написа́ть
I will write (start and finish) the letter.

Я бу́ду опи́сывать всё. опи́сывать
I will describe everything over time.

Брат опи́шет вы́ставку. описа́ть
(My) brother will describe the exhibition (completely).

Он встаёт ра́но ка́ждый день. вставáть
He gets up early every day [imperfective].

Вчера́ он встал о́чень по́здно. встать
Yesterday he got up very late [once, completed: perfective].

За́втра он вста́нет . . . встать
Tomorrow he will be getting up [one time: perfective] . . .

Ле́том он бу́дет вставáть . . . вставáть
During the summer he will get up [every day: imperfective future] . . .

Я забы́л бума́жник до́ма. забы́ть
I forgot my wallet at home [this one time: perfective past].

Он всегда́ всё забывáет. забывáть
He always forgets everything [all the time: imperfective].

Он всё де́лает о́чень бы́стро. де́лать
He does everything very quickly [everything, all the time: imperfective].

Он сде́лает э́то за́втра. сде́лать
He will do this tomorrow [one time, tomorrow: perfective future].

B. Sample Sentences: Daily Activities

Е́сли за́втра бу́дет хоро́шая пого́да, я пойду́ гуля́ть в парк.	If the weather is good tomorrow, I will go to the park for a walk.
Ве́чером я бу́ду сиде́ть до́ма.	I'll stay home in the evening.
Мой брат то́же бу́дет до́ма за́втра.	My brother will also be home tomorrow.
Мы бу́дем писа́ть пи́сьма роди́телям.	We'll write letters to our parents.
Я напишу́ письмо́ моему́ дру́гу.	I'll write a letter to my friend.
Брат напи́шет письмо́ сестре́ в Ме́ксику.	(My) brother will write a letter to (our) sister in Mexico.
Я бу́ду опи́сывать всё, что мы ви́дели в Москве́.	I'll describe everything we saw in Moscow.
Брат опи́шет худо́жественную вы́ставку.	(My) brother will describe the art exhibition.
За́втра у́тром мы пойдём в музе́й.	Tomorrow morning we'll go to the museum.
По доро́ге мы зайдём за мои́м дру́гем.	On the way we'll drop by to pick up my friend.
Он бу́дет нас ждать.	He'll wait for us.
Пусть подождёт. Я жда́ла его́ мно́го раз!	Let him wait. I've waited for him many times!
Я бы́стро помо́юсь, оде́нусь и причешу́сь.	I'll wash (myself), dress (myself), and comb my hair quickly.

Я всегда́ бы́стро мо́юсь, одева́юсь и причёсываюсь.	I always wash (myself), dress (myself), and comb my hair quickly.
Он встаёт ра́но ка́ждый день.	He gets up [rises] early every day.
Вчера́ он встал о́чень по́здно.	Yesterday he got up very late.
За́втра он вста́нет, как всегда́, ра́но.	Tomorrow he will get up early, as always.
Ле́том он бу́дет встава́ть в во́семь часо́в.	In the summer he will be getting up at eight o'clock.
Скажи́те ему́, что я бу́ду у него́ за́втра.	Tell him that I'll be at his house [by him] tomorrow.

C. More Verb Practice

Он всегда́ всё забыва́ет.	He always forgets everything.
По́езд отхо́дит в два часа́.	The train leaves at two o'clock.
Сего́дня он отойдёт в три часа́.	Today it will leave at three o'clock.
По́езд отошёл во́время.	The train left on time.
Вы говори́те сли́шком бы́стро. Я вас не понима́ю.	You talk too fast. I don't understand you.
Е́сли вы ска́жете всё э́то ме́дленно, я вас пойму́.	If you say all that slowly, I'll understand you.
Мы прочтём меню́ и пото́м зака́жем обе́д.	We'll read the menu and then order dinner.

Официа́нт ско́ро принесёт суп.	The waiter will bring the soup soon.
Я не могу́ бо́льше ждать.	I can't wait any longer.
Он смо́жет э́то сде́лать, е́сли полу́чит всё, что ему́ ну́жно.	He'll be able to do that if he gets everything he needs.

QUIZ 20

1. За́втра у́тром мы _____ в музе́й.	Tomorrow morning we'll go to the museum.
2. Я всегда́ бы́стро _____.	I always wash (myself) quickly.
3. Я бы́стро _____ и _____ в шко́лу.	I'll wash (myself) quickly and go to school.
4. Он _____ ра́но ка́ждый день.	He gets up early every day.
5. За́втра он _____. как всегда́, ра́но.	Tomorrow he will get up early, as usual.
6. Ле́том он _____ в во́семь часо́в.	In the summer he will be getting up at eight o'clock.
7. Е́сли вы _____ всё э́то ме́дленно, я вас пойму́.	If you say all that slowly, I will (be able to) understand you.
8. Официа́нт ско́ро _____ суп.	The waiter will bring the soup soon.
9. По́езд _____ во́время.	The train left on time.
10. Я не могу́ _____ ждать.	I can't wait any longer.

ANSWERS

1. пойдём; 2. мо́юсь; 3. помо́юсь, пойду́; 4. встаёт; 5. вста́нет; 6. бу́дет встава́ть; 7. ска́жете; 8. принесёт; 9. отошёл; 10. бо́льше.

LESSON 30

A. Introductions

Кто там?	Who's there?
Мóжно войти́?	May I come in?
Входи́те, пожáлуйста.	Please come in.
Позвóльте вам предстáвить моегó дрýга.	Allow me to introduce my friend to you.
Óчень рад с вáми познакóмиться.	I'm very glad to meet you [to become acquainted with you].
Óчень прия́тно.	Delighted. [Very pleasant.]
Разреши́те предстáвиться.	Allow me to introduce myself.
Меня́ зовýт Ивáн Петрóвич Крылóв.	My name is [they call me] Ivan Petrovich Krilov.
Сади́тесь, пожáлуйста.	Please have a seat.
Мóжно вам предложи́ть чáю?	May I offer you some tea?
Вы хоти́те со мной поговори́ть?	You want to speak with me?
Что вам нýжно?	What do you need?

B. At the Train Station

Скажи́те мне, пожáлуйста, где вокзáл?	Please tell me where the train station is.
Иди́те пря́мо до углá, потóм налéво оди́н квартáл.	Go straight to the corner, then one block to the left.

Где продаю́т биле́ты?	Where do they sell tickets?
Вон там ка́сса.	There's the ticket office.
Бо́же мой! Кака́я больша́я о́чередь!	Good heavens! What a long line!
Не беспоко́йтесь.	Don't worry.
О́чередь идёт о́чень бы́стро.	The line moves quickly.
Да́йте мне, пожа́луйста, биле́т в Я́сную Поля́ну.	Please give me a ticket to Yasnaya Polyana.
Вам в одну́ сто́рону и́ли туда́ и обра́тно?	Do you want a one-way ticket or a round trip?
Туда́ и обра́тно, пожа́луйста.	Round trip, please.
Когда́ отхо́дит по́езд? Да́йте мне, пожа́луйста, расписа́ние поездо́в.	When does the train leave? Give me a timetable, please.
Поезда́ в Я́сную Поля́ну отхо́дят ка́ждый час.	Trains to Yasnaya Polyana leave every hour.
Где аэропо́рт?	Where is the airport?
Аэропо́рт о́чень далеко́.	The airport is very far away.
Туда́ ну́жно е́хать и́ли авто́бусом, и́ли на такси́.	You have to take a bus or a taxi to get there.
Вот э́ти такси́ е́дут то́лько в аэропо́рт.	[Here] these taxis go only to the airport.
Туда́ по кра́йней ме́ре полчаса́ езды́.	It's at least a half-hour trip.
В аэропорту́, пре́жде чем сесть на самолёт, ну́жно получи́ть поса́дочный тало́н.	At the airport you have to get a boarding pass before you can get on the plane.

Пойдёмте! Уже́ о́чень по́здно.	Let's go. It's very late already.
Я не люблю́ опа́здывать.	I don't like to be late.
Э́то такси́ свобо́дно?	Is this taxi available?
Нам ну́жно в аэропо́рт.	We have to go to the airport.
Сади́тесь, пожа́луйста!	Get in, please.

C. In Case of Illness

Есть ли здесь в гости́нице до́ктор?	Is there a doctor in the hotel?
У меня́ о́чень боля́т голова́ и го́рло.	I have a bad headache and sore throat.
У меня́ на́сморк.	I have a head cold.
У меня́ боля́т зу́бы.	I have a toothache.
У него́ боли́т спина́.	His back hurts.
У неё температу́ра (жар).	She has a fever.
Нет ли у вас слаби́тельного?	Do you have a laxative?
Я о́чень пло́хо сплю.	I sleep very poorly.
Глаза́, у́ши, го́рло, нос, грудь, бок, ру́ки, но́ги; па́льцы на рука́х, па́льцы на нога́х.	Eyes, ears, throat, nose, chest (breast), side, hands (arms), feet (legs), fingers, toes.
Голова́ кру́жится.	I am dizzy [my head is spinning].
У вас температу́ра (жар).	You have a fever.
Боли́т живо́т.	My stomach aches.
Боль в желу́дке.	A pain in the stomach.
Мне ну́жно лежа́ть в посте́ли?	Do I have to stay in bed?

Да, обяза́тельно.	Yes, definitely.
Меня́ тошни́т.	I am nauseous.
Принима́йте э́то лека́рство четы́ре ра́за в день по столо́вой ло́жке.	Take a tablespoon of this medicine four times a day.
Но́чью сде́лайте себе́ согрева́ющий компре́сс.	At night apply a hot compress.
Ну́жно ли полоска́ть го́рло, до́ктор?	Should I gargle, doctor?
Да. Возьми́те одну́ ча́йную ло́жку со́ли на стака́н горя́чей воды́ и полощи́те по кра́йней ме́ре три ра́за в день: ка́ждые четы́ре часа́.	Yes. Add one teaspoon of salt to a glass of hot water and gargle at least three times a day, every four hours.
Не выходи́те, пока́ у вас не бу́дет норма́льная температу́ра.	Don't go out until your temperature is normal.

QUIZ 21

1. Мо́жно вам предложи́ть ча́ю?	a. Ivan Krilov knows the city well.
2. Меня́ зову́т Ива́н Крыло́в.	b. I don't like to be late.
3. Скажи́те мне, пожа́луйста, где вокза́л?	c. Do you want a one-way or a round-trip (ticket)?
4. Бо́же мой! Кака́я больша́я о́чередь!	d. May I offer you some tea?
5. Ива́н Крыло́в хорошо́ зна́ет го́род.	e. My name is Ivan Krilov.
6. Вам в одну́ сто́рону или туда́ и обра́тно?	f. It's at least a half-hour trip.
7. Поезда́ отхо́дят ка́ждый час.	g. Don't worry. The line is moving quickly.

8. Туда́ по кра́йней ме́ре полчаса́ езды́.
9. Я не люблю́ опа́здывать.
10. Не беспоко́йтесь, о́чередь идёт о́чень бы́стро.

h. Please tell me where the train station is.
i. Trains leave every hour.
j. Good heavens! What a long line!

ANSWERS
1—d; 2—e; 3—h; 4—j; 5—a; 6—c; 7—i; 8—f; 9—b; 10—g.

LESSON 31

A. Moscow Theatres

Ива́н:
Е́сли бы я знал, что сего́дня идёт в моско́вских теа́трах, я бы пошёл в теа́тр.

Véra:
Есть така́я ма́ленькая кни́жечка, кото́рая называ́ется «Репертуа́р моско́вских теа́тров».

Ива́н:
Где её мо́жно купи́ть?

Véra:
Во всех кни́жных кио́сках.

Ива́н:
Е́сли бы я знал э́то ра́ньше, то давно́ бы купи́л её.

Ivan:
If I knew what's playing in the Moscow theatres today, I would go to the theatre.

Vera:
There is a small book called *Program [Repertoire] of the Moscow Theatres.*

Ivan:
Where can one buy it?

Vera:
At all book stands.

Ivan:
If I had known that before [earlier], I would have bought it a long time ago.

Ве́ра:
Ну, вот ви́дите. Всё узнаётся в своё вре́мя.

Ива́н:
В москве́ мно́го теа́тров?

Ве́ра:
Да! О́чень мно́го! Дава́йте посмо́трим. Вот Большо́й теа́тр. Там иду́т о́перы и бале́т.

Ива́н:
Где он нахо́дится?

Ве́ра:
На Театра́льной пло́щади. Пото́м есть филиа́л Большо́го теа́тра, на Пу́шкинской улице. Э́то то́же о́перный теа́тр.

Ива́н:
А где нахо́дится Моско́вский Худо́жественный теа́тр?

Ве́ра:
На прое́зде Худо́жественного Теа́тра. Там иду́т то́лько дра́мы и коме́дии. Пото́м есть Ма́лый теа́тр, теа́тр и́мени Вахта́нгова,

Vera:
There, you see. In time one learns everything.

Ivan:
Are there many theatres in Moscow?

Vera:
Yes. Very many. Let's look (at the book). Here is the Bolshoi Theatre. Operas and ballet play there.

Ivan:
Where is it?

Vera:
On Theatre Square. Then there's an affiliate of the Bolshoi Theatre on Pushkin Street. This is also an opera theatre.

Ivan:
And where is the Moscow Art Theatre?

Vera:
On Art Theatre Lane. Only dramas and comedies play there. Then there's the Maliy Theatre, the theatre named after Vahktangov, the

теа́тр Опере́тты и т.д., и т.д.

Theatre of Operetta, etc., etc.

Ива́н:

В Москве́ есть цирк?

Ivan:

Is there a circus in Moscow?

Ве́ра:

Ещё бы! Коне́чно есть. И како́й ещё замеча́тельный! Обяза́тельно пойди́те в цирк. Ста́рый цирк нахо́дится на Цветно́м бульва́ре, дом 13. А но́вое зда́ние ци́рка на проспе́кте Верна́дского. А мо́жно ли доста́ть биле́ты на сего́дня, я не зна́ю. Ну́жно позвони́ть им по телефо́ну. Вот их но́мер: 212-16-40.

Vera:

And how! Of course there is! And what an excellent one! Go to the circus without fail. The old circus is on Flower Boulevard, No. 13. But the new circus building is on Vernadsky Prospect. I don't know if it's possibly to get tickets for today. You should (it is necessary to) call them (on the telephone). Here's their number: 212-16-40.

Ива́н:

Алло́, алло́. Скажи́те, пожа́луйста, есть биле́ты на сего́дня? Нет? Почему? Ах, у вас сего́дня выходно́й. Как жаль . . . Сего́дня нет представле́ния. Ну, вот ви́дите как мне везёт.

Ivan:

Hello, hello. Do you have tickets for today? No? Why? Oh, you're closed today [today is your day off]. What a pity . . . There's no performance today. There, you see; that's my luck.

Ве́ра:
Вы мо́жете пойти́ за́втра.
Ива́н:
Нет, я уже́ не успе́ю.
Ве́ра:
Почему́? Ра́зве вы ско́ро уезжа́ете?
Ива́н:
Коне́чно. За́втра. Ах, е́сли бы я зна́л об э́том ра́ньше, е́сли бы мне сказа́ли э́то хотя́ бы неде́лю тому́ наза́д!
Ве́ра:
Е́сли бы я зна́ла, что вы ничего́ не зна́ете, я бы сказа́ла вам.

Ива́н:
Вы же зна́ете, что я иностра́нец! Отку́да же мне знать?
Ве́ра:
Ну, прости́те. Ну, не серди́тесь!
Ива́н:
Я не сержу́сь. Но мне всё же о́чень, о́чень жаль, что я не побыва́л в ци́рке. Я так люблю́ цирк.

Vera:
You can go tomorrow.

Ivan:
No, I won't have time.
Vera:
Why? Are you leaving soon?
Ivan:
Of course. Tomorrow. Ah, if I had known about this earlier, if someone had told me that at least a week ago!
Vera:
If I had known that you didn't know anything, I would have told you.
Ivan:
But you know that I'm a foreigner! How am I to know?
Vera:
Oh, well, forgive me. Now, don't be angry!
Ivan:
I'm not angry. But all the same I'm very, very sorry that I didn't get to the circus. I just love the circus.

Ве́ра:	*Vera:*
Ну, ничего́. В сле́дующий раз.	Well, that's okay. Next time.

B. Subjunctive and Conditional Moods

The conditional and subjunctive are likely to be among the most difficult grammatical constructions in any language. However, in Russian, they are the easiest. All you have to know is the particle бы, and that the past tense of the verb is used together with it.

е́сли бы	if
Если бы я знал,	If I knew, Had I known,
я пошёл бы.	I would have gone. I would go.
Я позвони́л бы, е́сли бы у меня́ был (бы) ваш телефо́н.	I would have called you, if I had your telephone number.

C. Word Study

просто́й	simple
взро́слый	adult
гость	guest
рубль	ruble
назва́ние	title
приглаша́ть-пригласи́ть	to invite
не́сколько	several
открыва́ть-откры́ть	to open
у́жин	supper
у́тро	morning

QUIZ 22

1. Ну, вот ви́дите. Всё узнаётся в своё вре́мя.	a. He speaks Russian very well.

2. Почему́? Ра́зве вы ско́ро уезжа́ете?
3. Сего́дня нет представле́ния.
4. Е́сли бы я знал э́то ра́ньше, то давно́ бы купи́л её.
5. О́чень мно́го. Дава́йте посмо́трим.
6. Он о́чень хорошо́ говори́т по-ру́сски.
7. В на́шем го́роде есть замеча́тельный цирк.
8. Где он нахо́дится?
9. Я о́чень люблю́ цирк и хожу́ туда́ о́чень ча́сто.
10. Моя́ сестра́ живёт и рабо́тает в ма́леньком го́роде.
11. Два дня тому́ наза́д я был в теа́тре.
12. В Моско́вском Худо́жественном теа́тре иду́т дра́мы и коме́дии.
13. А мно́го теа́тров в Москве́?
14. Он никогда́ ничего́ не зна́ет.
15. Она́ не зна́ла, что сего́дня э́тот магази́н закры́т.
16. Скажи́те, пожа́луйста, мо́жно ли получи́ть биле́ты на сего́дня?
17. Ну, вот ви́дите, как мне везёт.
18. Вы мо́жете пойти́ за́втра.
19. Ну, прости́те. Ну, не серди́тесь!
20. Ну, ничего́. В сле́дующий раз.

b. Are there many theatres in Moscow?
c. Where is it located?
d. I really love the circus and go there often.
e. I was at the theatre two days ago.
f. He never knows anything.
g. Tell me, please, is it possible to get tickets for today?
h. There, you see; that's my luck.
i. There's no performance today.
j. Oh, well, forgive me. Now, don't be annoyed!
k. There, you see. In time one learns everything.
l. Very many. Let's take a look.
m. She didn't know that this store is closed today.
n. We have an excellent circus in our town.
o. If I had known that before [earlier], I would have bought it a long time ago.
p. You can go tomorrow.
q. Dramas and comedies play at the Moscow Art Theatre.
r. My sister lives and works in a small town.
s. Well, that's okay. Next time.
t. Why? Are you leaving soon?

NOTE
Quizzes from this point on will include review sentences from previous lessons.

ANSWERS
1—k; 2—t; 3—i; 4—o; 5—l; 6—a; 7—n; 8—c; 9—d; 10—r; 11—e; 12—q; 13—b; 14—f; 15—m; 16—g; 17—h; 18—p; 19—j; 20—s.

LESSON 32

A. Useful Words and Expressions

Вот как!	Is that so!
Как бы не так!	Nothing of the sort!
Бу́дьте как до́ма!	Make yourself at home.
как ви́дно	as can be seen
Э́то как раз то, что мне ну́жно.	That's just what I need.
Э́то де́ло вку́са.	That's a matter of taste.
Соверше́нно ве́рно.	Quite right. [Absolutely.]
Ещё бы.	And how! You bet!
ко́е-как	anyhow; haphazardly
Он холосто́й.	He's a bachelor.
Он же́нится.	He is getting married.
Он жена́т.	He is married.
Она́ ещё не за́мужем.	She is still not married.
Она́ выхо́дит за́муж.	She is getting married.
Она́ за́мужем.	She is married.
(родно́й) брат	brother

(родна́я) сестра́	sister
двою́родный брат	(first) cousin (*m.*)
двою́родная сестра́	(first) cousin (*f.*)
смотре́ть в о́ба	keep one's eyes open: be on one's guard
Э́тому не помо́жешь.	It can't be helped.
пока́ что	in the meantime
Поговори́те с ним, пока́ он там.	Talk to [with] him while he is there.
Оста́вьте меня́ в поко́е.	Leave me alone [in peace].
Он про́сто ничего́ не зна́ет.	He simply knows nothing.
Он ничего́ не име́ет про́тив э́того.	He has nothing against it. [He doesn't mind.]
Она́ лю́бит пуска́ть пыль в глаза́.	She likes to show off [to put on airs].
Тру́дно рабо́тать на пусто́й желу́док.	It's difficult to work on an empty stomach.
Нам с ва́ми по пути́.	We're going your way.
У вас золото́е се́рдце.	You have a heart of gold.
Благодарю́ вас от всего́ се́рдца.	Thank you from the bottom of my heart.
С глаз доло́й, из се́рдца вон.	Out of sight, out of mind.
бежа́ть изо все́х сил	to run as fast as one can
крича́ть изо все́х сил	to scream at the top of one's voice
крича́ть во всё го́рло	
Он де́лает э́то по привы́чке.	He does it out of habit.
ле́гче сказа́ть, чем сде́лать	easier said than done
ска́зано–сде́лано	no sooner said than done
в ско́ром вре́мени	before long
ско́рая по́мощь	first aid

одни́м сло́вом	in a word; in short
други́ми слова́ми	in other words
Всё бу́дет забы́то.	Everything will be forgotten.
гла́вным о́бразом	mainly
таки́м о́бразом	in this way
на вся́кий слу́чай	just in case
во вся́ком слу́чае	in any case
в тако́м слу́чае	in this case

B. Telephone Calls

Отку́да мо́жно позвони́ть?	Where can I make a phone call?
Здесь есть телефо́нная бу́дка?	Is there a phone booth here?
Здесь есть телефо́нный спра́вочник?	Is there a telephone directory?
Опера́тор . . .	Operator . . .
Я хочу́ позвони́ть по э́тому но́меру.	I'd like to call this number.
Я хочу́ позвони́ть в Соединённые Шта́ты.	I'd like to call the United States.
Алло́.	Hello.
Говори́т . . .	This is . . .
Кто звони́т?	Who is calling?
С кем я говорю́?	To whom am I speaking?
Говори́те ме́дленно, пожа́луйста.	Speak slowly, please.
Э́то Андре́й.	This is Andrei.
Можно поговори́ть с Вади́мом?	May I speak with Vadim?
Мой но́мер . . .	My number is . . .

Как мне связа́ться с опера́тором?	How do I get the operator?
Меня́ разъедини́ли.	I was cut off.
Вы могли́ бы соедини́ть меня́ ещё раз?	Could you connect me again?
Я хоте́л бы поговори́ть с . . .	I'd like to speak to . . .
Скажи́те ему́, пожа́луйста, что я звони́л.	Please tell him I called.

C. Word Study

забыва́ть-забы́ть	to forget
пра́здник	holiday
оши́бка	mistake
хо́лодно	cold (adv.)
гру́стный	sad
прекра́сный	wonderful
хлеб	bread
остано́вка	stop
дверь	door

LESSON 33

A. More Verbs of Motion

Ходи́ть из одно́й ко́мнаты в другу́ю.	Walk from one room to another.
Е́здить из го́рода в го́род.	Travel from city to city.
Он хо́дит в библиоте́ку о́чень ча́сто.	He goes [walks] to the library very often.
Сего́дня мы идём в теа́тр.	Today we are going to the theatre.

Я всегда́ беру́ с собо́й бино́кль; я о́чень близору́кая.	I always take my glasses with me; I'm very nearsighted.
Мне не ну́жен бино́кль. Я дальнозо́ркий.	I don't need glasses. I'm farsighted.
Он взял кни́гу и ушёл.	He took the book and left.
Мой друг прие́хал вчера́ в Петербу́рг.	My friend arrived in Petersburg yesterday.
Он е́здит туда́ ка́ждое ле́то.	He goes there every summer.
Я уезжа́ю за́втра.	I'm leaving tomorrow.
Я уе́ду за́втра.	I'll leave tomorrow.
Я прие́ду во Владивосто́к то́лько че́рез во́семь дней.	I'll get to [arrive in] Vladivostok in only eight days.
Ско́лько вре́мени вы там бу́дете?	How long [how much time] will you be there?
Я ду́маю, что пробу́ду там о́коло двух неде́ль.	I think that I'll spend about two weeks there.
Я уже́ был оди́н раз во Владивосто́ке, но то́лько прое́здом по доро́ге в Аме́рику.	I've already been in Vladivostok once, but only [when] passing through on the way to America.
Я прилете́л из Сан-Франци́ско.	I flew from San Francisco.
Я хоте́л бы пое́хать в Калифо́рнию.	I would like to go to California.
Говоря́т, что там замеча́тельная приро́да.	They say that the scenery [nature] there is magnificent.

Почему́ же вы не е́дете?	Well, why don't you go?
У меня́ о́чень ма́ло свобо́дного вре́мени.	I have very little free time.
Вы мо́жете вы́ехать в нача́ле ма́я и провести́ там весь ию́нь.	You can leave at the beginning of May and spend all of June there.
Но я до́лжен прие́хать обра́тно в Росси́ю в конце́ ию́ня.	But I have to be back in Russia by the end of June.
Не бо́йтесь, вы успе́ете.	Don't worry, you'll make it.
Самолётом мо́жно путеше́ствовать о́чень бы́стро.	You can travel by plane very quickly.
Мо́жет быть, вы пра́вы. Попыта́юсь так и сде́лать.	Perhaps you're right. I'll try to do just that.

QUIZ 23

1. Бу́дьте как до́ма.	a. He goes there every summer.
2. Сего́дня мы идём в теа́тр.	b. Everything will be forgotten.
3. Он взял кни́гу и ушёл.	c. Where can I make a phone call?
4. Он е́здит туда́ ка́ждое ле́то.	d. Easier said than done.
5. Ско́лько вре́мени вы бу́дете там?	e. I'll try to do just that.
6. Всё бу́дет забы́то.	f. You can leave at the beginning of May.
7. У меня́ о́чень ма́ло свобо́дного вре́мени.	g. Make yourself at home.
8. Я был там по доро́ге домо́й.	h. Don't worry; you'll make it [you'll have time].

9. Говоря́т, что там замеча́тельная приро́да.
10. Отку́да мо́жно позвони́ть?
11. Соверше́нно ве́рно.
12. Ле́гче сказать, чем сде́лать.
13. Мо́жет быть, вы пра́вы.
14. Попыта́юсь так и сде́лать.
15. Он до́лжен прие́хать обра́тно в го́род в конце́ ию́ня.
16. Вы мо́жете вы́ехать в нача́ле ма́я.
17. Не бо́йтесь, вы успе́ете.
18. Она́ всегда́ берёт с собо́й свою́ сестру́.
19. Мо́жно поговори́ть с Вади́мом?
20. Оста́вьте меня́ в поко́е.

i. He has to be back in town by the end of June.
j. He took the book and left.
k. Today we are going to the theatre.
l. How long will you be there?
m. I have very little free time.
n. She always takes her sister with her.
o. Leave me alone.
p. May I speak with Vadim?
q. Perhaps you're right.
r. Quite right.
s. They say that the scenery [nature] there is magnificent.
t. I passed by [was] there on my way home.

ANSWERS
1—g; 2—k; 3—j; 4—a; 5—l; 6—b; 7—m; 8—t; 9—s; 10—c; 11—r; 12—d; 13—q; 14—e; 15—i; 16—f; 17—h; 18—n; 19—p; 20—o.

LESSON 34

A. Newspapers, Books, Radio, and Television

Я хочу́ купи́ть газе́ту. I want to buy a newspaper.

Я хочу́ купи́ть журна́л. I want to buy a magazine.

У вас есть кни́ги на англи́йском языке́?	Do you have any books in English?
Есть музыка́льная програ́мма?	Is there a music station?
Есть програ́мма новосте́й?	Is there a news station?
Есть програ́мма прогно́за пого́ды?	Is there a weather station?
Во ско́лько нача́ло переда́чи?	What time is the program?
У вас есть телевизио́нная програ́мма?	Do you have a television guide?
Во ско́лько прогно́з пого́ды?	When is the weather forecast?
По како́му кана́лу идёт переда́ча?	What channel is the program on?

B. At the Post Office

Я ищу́ Главпочта́мт.	I'm looking for the main post office.
Где нахо́дится ближа́йший почто́вый я́щик?	Where's the nearest mailbox?
Ско́лько сто́ит отпра́вить письмо́ в Соединенные Штаты Америки?	How much is it for a letter to the U.S.?
откры́тка	postcard
Я хочу́ купи́ть ма́рки.	I want to buy stamps.
Я хочу́ посла́ть э́ту посы́лку в Соединенные Штаты Америки.	I want to send this package to the United States.

Мо́жно посла́ть телегра́мму в Нью-Йо́рк?	Can I send a telegram to New York?
Ско́лько сто́ит одно́ сло́во?	How much is it per word?
Придёт ли она́ за́втра у́тром?	Will it arrive tomorrow morning?
Како́е окно́ для телегра́мм?	Which window is it for telegrams?

C. Meeting an Old Friend

Я е́хал из Петербу́рга в Москву́. По доро́ге по́езд останови́лся в Но́вгороде. Но́вгород не о́чень большо́й го́род, но тут есть прекра́сный вокза́л и очень хоро́ший рестора́н. По́езд стоит там це́лый час. Я вы́шел из по́езда и пошёл погуля́ть по платфо́рме, а пото́м реши́л пойти́ в рестора́н поесть. Как то́лько я вошёл в рестора́н, я встре́тил мою́ знако́мую из Москвы́.

I was on my way from Petersburg to Moscow. On the way, the train stopped in Novgorod. Novgorod is not a very large city, but there is a wonderful station there and a very good restaurant. The train was to be there for a whole hour. I got off the train and went for a stroll on the platform, and then I decided to go to the restaurant to eat. As soon as I walked into the restaurant, I met my friend from Moscow.

Серге́й:	*Sergei:*
Ве́ра Петро́вна, здра́вствуйте! Како́е интере́сное совпаде́ние!	Hello, Vera Petrovna! What an interesting coincidence.

Ве́ра:
А! Серге́й Никола́евич! Как я ра́да вас ви́деть!

Серге́й:
Что вы здесь де́лаете? Куда́ вы е́дете?

Ве́ра:
Я е́ду в Приба́лтику. У меня́ о́тпуск.

Серге́й:
Вы полу́чите большо́е удово́льствие.

Приба́лтика прекра́сна.

Ве́ра:
Да, я зна́ю. Я так мно́го слы́шала и так мно́го чита́ла о мо́ре и сосно́вых леса́х. Я про́сто не могу́ дожда́ться той мину́ты, когда́ пе́редо мно́й бу́дет мо́ре.

Серге́й:
Ну тепе́рь уже́ не до́лго ждать. От Но́вгорода о́чень бли́зко. Давно́ вы из Москвы́?

Vera:
Ah, Sergei Nicholaevich! How glad I am to see you!

Sergei:
What are you doing here? Where are you going?

Vera:
I'm going to the Baltics. I'm on vacation.

Sergei:
You'll enjoy yourself greatly [receive great pleasure].

The Baltic area is magnificent.

Vera:
Yes, I know. I've heard so much and read so much about the sea and pine forests. I simply can't wait for the moment when I'll see the sea before me.

Sergei:
Well, now you won't have to wait long. It's very close to Novgorod. Are you away from Moscow very long?

Ве́ра:
Нет, то́лько три дня. Я вы́ехала в суббо́ту у́тром.
Серге́й:
Вы ви́дели моего́ бра́та пе́ред отъе́здом?

Vera:
No, only three days. I left Saturday morning.
Sergei:
Did you see my brother before leaving?

Ве́ра:
Да, коне́чно, я зашла́ к нему́ в четве́рг ве́чером, но его́ не́ бы́ло до́ма.
Серге́й:
Зна́чит вы его́ не ви́дели?
Ве́ра:
Нет, почему́ же? Я оста́вила ему́ запи́ску, и он позвони́л мне на сле́дующий день и пото́м пришёл ко мне.
Серге́й:
Как там всё в Москве? Всё в поря́дке?

Vera:
Yes, of course, I dropped in on him Thursday evening, but he wasn't home.
Sergei:
So [that means] you didn't see him?
Vera:
No, why? I left him a note, and he called me the next day and then came to see me.

Sergei:
How's everything in Moscow? Everything all right?

Ве́ра:
Всё норма́льно. Жена́ ва́шего бра́та была́ больна́, но она́ уже́ попра́вилась и чу́вствует себя́ непло́хо.
Серге́й:
Да, я зна́ю. Брат мне писа́л, и я о́чень

Vera:
Everything's fine. Your brother's wife was sick, but she has recovered and feels quite well.
Sergei:
Yes, I know. My brother wrote me,

волнова́лся.

and I was very worried.

Ве́ра:

Когда́ вы прие́дете в Москву́, пожа́луйста, позвони́те ма́ме и скажи́те, что встре́тили меня́. Вот она́ удиви́тся! Серге́й Никола́евич, а вы уже́ обе́дали?

Vera:

When you arrive in Moscow, please call my mother and say that you ran into me. She'll be so surprised. Sergei Nicholaevich, have you already eaten?

Серге́й:

Нет, коне́чно нет, пойдёмте вме́сте и переку́сим.

Sergei:

No, of course not. Let's go and have a bite together.

Ве́ра:

Вот хорошо́, а то я про́сто умира́ю с го́лоду.

Vera:

That's good, I'm simply dying of hunger.

Серге́й:

Вот здесь свобо́дный сто́лик. Дава́йте ся́дем здесь. Когда́ вы бу́дете в Ри́ге, не забу́дьте подня́ться на Пороховую Ба́шню.

Sergei:

Here's an empty table. Let's sit here. When you're in Riga, don't forget to go up to the top of the fortress tower.

Ве́ра:

Говоря́т, что э́то о́чень интере́сно. Э́то о́чень ста́рое зда́ние, пра́вда?

Vera:

They say that it's very interesting. It is a very old building, right?

Серге́й:

Соверше́нно ве́рно. И вы зна́ете, отту́да открыва́ется

Sergei:

Quite right. And you know, from there, there is [opens up]

изуми́тельный вид на весь го́род.	an amazing view of the whole city.
Ве́ра:	*Vera:*
Мне да́же не ве́рится, что я всё э́то уви́жу.	I can hardly believe [even don't believe] that I will see all this.

За обе́дом я рассказа́л Ве́ре Петро́вне всё, что я знал о Приба́лтике: куда́ лу́чше всего́ пойти́, что посмотре́ть, где мо́жно хорошо́ пое́сть. Час прошёл о́чень бы́стро, и я чуть не опозда́л на свой по́езд. Я вскочи́л в по́езд уже́ по́сле тре́тьего звонка́.

At dinner I told Vera Petrovna all that I knew about the Baltics: the best places to go, what to see, and the good places to eat. The hour passed very quickly, and I was almost late for my train. I jumped on the train after the third bell had already rung.

LESSON 35

A. End of the Vacation

Как бы́стро лети́т вре́мя!	How quickly time flies.
Вот уже́ четы́ре неде́ли с тех пор, как я нача́л путеше́ствовать.	[Here] it's four weeks already since I started to travel.
К сожале́нию, мой о́тпуск подхо́дит к концу́.	Unfortunately my vacation is coming to an end.
Мне ну́жно собира́ться.	I have to start packing.

У меня́ три чемода́на.	I have three suitcases.
Оди́н о́чень большо́й и два други́х поме́ньше.	One is very big, and the other two somewhat smaller.
В большо́й чемода́н помеща́ется о́чень мно́го вещей.	A great many things can be put into the big suitcase.
Но зато́ его́ о́чень тяжело́ нести́.	But on the other hand, it's very heavy to carry.
К сча́стью, мой друг пое́дет со мно́й на вокза́л.	Luckily, my friend will go to the station with me.
Он о́чень си́льный.	He's very strong.
Ему́ всё легко́.	Everything is light for him.
Ну́жно бу́дет купи́ть биле́ты зара́нее, что́бы не стоя́ть в о́череди.	I'll have to buy tickets beforehand in order not to stand in line [in turn].
Ну́жно не забы́ть позвони́ть всем знако́мым.	I [one] must not forget to telephone all my friends.
Ну́жно бу́дет попроща́ться со все́ми.	I'll have to say goodbye to [take leave of] all of them.
Я сде́лала о́чень мно́го сни́мков и отдала́ их прояви́ть.	I took many pictures and left [gave] them to be developed.
Наде́юсь, что все фотогра́фии бу́дут гото́вы до моего́ отъе́зда.	I hope that all the pictures will be ready before my departure.
Я ещё не получи́ла бельё из сти́рки.	I still haven't gotten back my laundry.

Оно́ должно́ быть уже́ гото́во.	It should be ready by now.
Ну, вот ве́щи уже́ уло́жены.	Well, my things are all packed.
За́втра мы е́дем домо́й. Коне́ц о́тпуску. До сле́дующего го́да.	Tomorrow we are going home. End of my vacation. Until next year.
В бу́дущем году́ мы опя́ть собира́емся пое́хать куда́-нибудь.	We are planning to go somewhere again next year.
Мне о́чнь хо́чется пое́хать в Сре́днюю А́зию.	I'd very much like to go to Central Asia.
Говоря́т, что там о́чень интере́сно.	They say [it is said] that it's very interesting there.
Там мно́го стари́нных городо́в.	There are many old cities there.
Наприме́р, го́род Ташке́нт де́лится на ста́рый го́род и но́вый го́род. Э́тот го́род изве́стен уже́ с седьмо́го ве́ка.	For instance, the city Tashkent is divided into the Old City and the New City. This city dates back to [is known from] the seventh century.
Там есть па́мятники дре́вней архитекту́ры пятна́дцатого и шестна́дцатого веко́в.	There are relics of ancient architecture of the fifteenth and sixteenth centuries.

QUIZ 24

1. Я про́сто не могу́ дожда́ться той мину́ты, когда́ пе́редо мной бу́дет мо́ре.
2. В э́том го́роде есть прекра́сный вокза́л и о́чень хоро́ший рестора́н.
3. Како́е интере́сное совпаде́ние!
4. Когда́ я вошёл в рестора́н, я встре́тил мою́ знако́мую.
5. Вот свобо́дный сто́лик.
6. Говоря́т, что э́то о́чень интере́сно.
7. Дава́йте ся́дем здесь.
8. Отту́да открыва́ется изуми́тельный вид на весь го́род.
9. По́езд стои́т здесь це́лый час.
10. Мне да́же не ве́рится, что я всё э́то уви́жу.
11. Пожа́луйста, позвони́те мое́й сестре́ и скажи́те, что вы встре́тили меня́.
12. Я чуть не опозда́л на свой по́езд.
13. Как бы́стро лети́т вре́мя!
14. Я хочу́ купи́ть газе́ту.
15. К сча́стью, мой друг пое́дет со мной на вокза́л.
16. Ну́жно не забы́ть позвони́ть всем знако́мым.
17. Ско́лько сто́ит отпра́вить письмо́?
18. В бу́дущем году́ мы опя́ть

a. They say that it's very interesting.
b. From there, there is [opens up] an amazing view of the whole city.
c. I was almost late for my train.
d. The train stops here for a whole hour.
e. I want to buy a newspaper.
f. I must not forget to telephone all my friends.
g. Please call my sister and tell her that you met me.
h. How quickly time flies!
i. Luckily, my friend will go to the station with me.
j. How much is it for a letter?
k. They say that it's very interesting there.
l. Next year we will go somewhere again.
m. This city dates back to [is known from] the seventh century.
n. Let's sit here.
o. What an interesting coincidence!
p. Here's an empty table.
q. I simply can't wait for the moment when I'll see the sea before [in front of] me.
r. I can hardly believe that

поéдем кудá-нибудь.
19. Говорят, что там óчень интерéсно.
20. Э́тот гóрод извéстен ужé с седьмóго вéка.

I will see all this.
s. In this city there is a wonderful station and a very good restaurant.
t. When I walked into the restaurant, I met my friend.

ANSWERS
1—q; 2—s; 3—o; 4—t; 5—p; 6—a; 7—n; 8—b; 9—d; 10—r; 11—g; 12—c; 13—h; 14—e; 15—i; 16—f; 17—j; 18—l; 19—k; 20—m.

LESSON 36

A. May or Can

The words "may" and "may not," and "can" and "cannot" are expressed in Russian by мóжно (it is possible) and нельзя́ (it is not possible).

Мóжно вы́йти?	May I go out?
Нет, нельзя́.	No, you may not.

Нельзя́ is a Russian word for which there is no exact English equivalent.

Мóжно?	**Нельзя́**
May I?	No, you may not.
Can I?	No, you cannot.
Is it possible?	It is impossible.
Is it allowed?	It is not allowed.

Нельзя́ сказáть, что здесь жáрко.	You would not say that it is hot here.
Здесь нельзя́ кури́ть.	You (one) cannot (may not) smoke here.

Мо́жно and нельзя́ are adverbs and therefore do not change their form.

B. May I?

Са́ша:
Здесь мо́жно кури́ть?
Ми́ша:
Нет, здесь нельзя́ кури́ть. Посмотри́те, вот там напи́сано: «Кури́ть воспреща́ется».
Са́ша:
А где вообще́ мо́жно кури́ть?
Ми́ша:
В теа́трах мо́жно кури́ть в фойе́. В поезда́х есть специа́льные ваго́ны для куря́щих.
Са́ша:
У меня́ нет спи́чек. Да́йте мне, пожа́луйста, спи́чки. Ру́сские сигаре́ты совсе́м не таки́е, как америка́нские. К ним на́до привы́кнуть.
Ми́ша:
Куре́ние вообще́ о́чень плоха́я привы́чка.

Sasha:
May one smoke here?
Misha:
No, (there's) no smoking here. Look, the sign says [it's written there]: "Smoking forbidden."
Sasha:
Where can one smoke?
Misha:
In theatres one may smoke in the lobby. In trains there are special cars for smokers.
Sasha:
I have no matches. Please give me matches. Russian cigarettes are not at all like American (cigarettes). One must get used to them.
Misha:
Smoking is, in general, a very bad habit.

Са́ша:
Соверше́нно с ва́ми согла́сен, но я о́чень люблю́ кури́ть.
Ми́ша:
Вы уже́ вы́курили всю па́чку. Хва́тит на сего́дня.
Са́ша:
Ничего́ подо́бного. Я вы́курил то́лько полпа́чки.
Ми́ша:
Пе́йте бо́льше молока́. Э́то вам о́чень поле́зно.
Са́ша:
Я не люблю́ пить и есть то, что поле́зно.

Ми́ша:
Вы что хоти́те, то и де́лаете!
Са́ша:
Коне́чно! Что хочу́, то и де́лаю.
Ми́ша:
Кури́ть мно́го–вре́дно, а пить мно́го молока́ поле́зно.

Са́ша:
Мо́жет бы́ть э́то и так, но я не люблю́ молоко́.

Sasha:
I completely agree with you, but I love to smoke.
Misha:
You've already finished a whole pack. Enough for today.
Sasha:
Nothing of the sort. I smoked only half a pack.
Misha:
Drink more milk. It's very good for you.

Sasha:
I don't like to drink and eat the things that are good for me.
Misha:
You do whatever you want!
Sasha:
Of course! What I want (to do), I do.
Misha:
Smoking a lot is harmful, but drinking a lot of milk is good for you.
Sasha:
Maybe that's so, but I don't like milk.

Ми́ша:
Все де́ти выраста́ют на молоке́.
Са́ша:
Когда́ я был ребёнком, я пил молоко́, а тепе́рь я курю́.
Ми́ша:
Вы свобо́дный челове́к. Де́лайте, что хоти́те.

Misha:
All children grow up on milk.
Sasha:
When I was a baby I drank milk, and now I smoke.
Misha:
You're a free person. Do as you please.

C. I CAN'T

Мне нельзя́ выходи́ть. Я простуди́лся. У меня́ боля́т го́рло и голова́.
I can't go out. I caught a cold. I have a sore throat and a headache.

У вас на́сморк. Вам на́до лежа́ть в посте́ли. До́ктор сказа́л, что вам нельзя́ кури́ть.
You have a head cold. You have to stay in bed. The doctor said that you can't smoke.

На э́тот конце́рт нельзя́ попа́сть: все биле́ты про́даны.
It's impossible to get to that concert. All the tickets have been sold.

О́чень жа́ль, что нельзя́. Пойдём куда́-нибудь в друго́е ме́сто.
Too bad that we can't go. Let's go somewhere else.

Ему́ нельзя́ ходи́ть по ле́стнице. У него́ сла́бое се́рдце.
He can't take the stairs. He has a weak heart.

Он живёт как нельзя́ лу́чше.
He can't live any better than he does.

Где ваш друг Никола́й сего́дня?	Where is your friend Nicholas today?
Я никогда́ не зна́ю, где он.	I never know where he is [could be].

QUIZ 25

1. Вы что хоти́те, то и де́лаете.
2. Кури́ть мно́го вре́дно, а пить мно́го молока́ поле́зно.
3. Нельзя́ сказа́ть, что э́то всегда́ так.
4. На э́тот конце́рт нельзя́ попа́сть: все биле́ты про́даны.
5. Ему́ нельзя́ ходи́ть по ле́стнице. У него́ сла́бое се́рдце.
6. Он живёт, как нельзя́ лу́чше.
7. От кого́ вы получи́ли письмо́?
8. С кем вы бы́ли в теа́тре вчера́?
9. Что зна́чит э́то сло́во?
10. Чего́ то́лько нет в э́том магази́не!
11. Не понима́ю—о чём тут говори́ть?
12. Как вы себя́ чу́вствуете?
13. У них есть всё, что вам ну́жно.
14. Мне хо́чется пить.
15. Я могу́ сказа́ть то́лько не́сколько слов по-ру́сски.

a. They have everything you need.
b. What does this word mean?
c. I can say only a few words in Russian.
d. What they don't have in this store!
e. You pronounce Russian words badly.
f. I don't understand—what is there to talk about?
g. I'm thirsty.
h. What kind of wine do you want—white or red?
i. Excuse me, but I don't understand you.
j. Where are you going to have dinner after work?
k. You do whatever you want.
l. It's difficult for me to understand when you speak so fast.
m. He can't live any better than he does.
n. With whom were you in the theatre yesterday?
o. Smoking a lot is harmful, but drinking a lot of milk is good for you.

16. Вы пло́хо произно́сите ру́сские слова́.
17. Мне тру́дно понима́ть, когда́ вы говори́те так бы́стро.
18. Прости́те, но я не понима́ю вас.
19. Како́е вино́ вы хоти́те—бе́лое и́ли кра́сное?
20. Куда́ вы идёте обе́дать по́сле рабо́ты?

p. From whom did you get a letter?
q. It's impossible to get to that concert. All the tickets have been sold.
r. He can't take the stairs. He has a weak heart.
s. How are you feeling?
t. You [one] can't say that it is always so.

ANSWERS
1—k; 2—o; 3—t; 4—q; 5—r; 6—m; 7—p; 8—n; 9—b; 10—d; 11—f; 12—s; 13—a; 14—g; 15—c; 16—e; 17—l; 18—i; 19—h; 20—j.

LESSON 37

A. Lost and Found

Мы не зна́ли доро́ги и потеря́ли мно́го вре́мени по доро́ге в музе́й.	We didn't know the way and lost a lot of time on the way to the museum.
Он потеря́л свой бума́жник.	He lost his wallet.
Об э́том ну́жно заяви́ть милиционе́ру и́ли пря́мо в мили́цию.	You must report that to a policeman or go directly to the police station.
Е́сли кто́-нибудь найдёт э́тот бума́жник, то его́, по всей вероя́тности, верну́т.	If someone finds this wallet, he will, in all probability, return it.
Она́ ничего́ никогда́ не теря́ет.	She never loses anything.

Вчера́ она́ потеря́ла одну́ перча́тку.	Yesterday she lost one glove.
Кто́-то её нашёл.	Someone found it.
Она́ лежи́т тепе́рь на столе́ у администра́тора гости́ницы.	It's now at the hotel manager's desk.
Когда́ я хожу́ пешко́м по у́лице, я всегда́ что́-нибудь нахожу́.	When I walk along the street, I always find something.
Сего́дня я нашёл о́чень хоро́шую автору́чку.	Today I found a very good fountain pen.
Мне так жаль того́, кто её потеря́л.	I'm so sorry for the person who lost it.
Что вы и́щете?	What are you looking for?
Я всегда́ что́-нибудь ищу́.	I'm always looking for something.
Ищи́те–и вы найдёте.	Seek, and you will find.
В Москве́ не тру́дно найти́ хоро́ший теа́тр.	In Moscow it's not difficult to find a good theatre.
Я потеря́лся и не знал, куда́ идти́.	I lost my way and didn't know where to go.
Я потеря́лся и не знал, что сказа́ть.	I became flustered and didn't know what to say.
Я заблуди́лся и не мог найти́ доро́ги.	I got lost and couldn't find the way.
В э́том горо́де о́чень не тру́дно заблуди́ться.	It's not hard to lose one's way in this city.
Э́то о́чень ста́рый го́род. У́лицы у́зкие	This is a very old city. The streets are

и краси́вые, и никогда́ не изве́стно, куда́ у́лица повернёт и куда́ она́ вас приведёт.

narrow and beautiful, and you never know where the street turns and where it will lead you.

Ма́ленькие у́зкие у́лицы называ́ются по-ру́сски переу́лками.

Little narrow streets are called "pereulok" in Russian.

В го́роде, где я когда́-то жил, была́ у́лица, кото́рая называ́лась «Театра́льный переу́лок».

In the city where I lived one time, there was a street that was called "Theatre Pereulok" [Theatre Lane].

Е́сли переу́лок не проходно́й, то он называ́ется тупико́м.

If a pereulok has a dead end, it is called a "tupik."

О́чень ча́сто говоря́т: «Я попа́л в тупи́к» Э́то зна́чит, что вы в тако́м положе́нии, из кото́рого нет вы́хода. Наде́юсь, что никто́ из нас никогда́ не попадёт в тупи́к.

Very often it is said: "I got into a tupik." This means that you are in the kind of situation that has no way out. I hope that not one of us ever falls into a tupik.

Из ка́ждого тупика́ мо́жно вы́йти тем же путём, каки́м вы в него́ ришли́.

It is possible to get out of every tupik by the same road through which you entered.

Иногда́ ну́жно сде́лать шаг наза́д. Все мы де́лаем иногда́ оши́бки.

Sometimes it is necessary to take a step backward. We all make mistakes sometimes.

Не ошиба́ется то́лько тот, кто ничего́ не де́лает.	Only he who does nothing makes no mistakes.
Я оши́бся и пошёл напра́во, а на́до бы́ло идти́ нале́во.	I made a mistake and turned to the right, and I should have gone to the left.
О́чень тру́дно говори́ть без оши́бок.	It's very difficult to speak without mistakes.
О́чень тру́дно писа́ть без оши́бок.	It's very difficult to write without mistakes.
Легко́ де́лать то́лько то, что вы хорошо́ зна́ете.	It's only easy to do that which you know well.
Рабо́тайте, занима́йтесь, слу́шайте, повторя́йте, чита́йте, запомина́йте.	Work, study, listen, repeat, read, memorize.
Вы́учите всё, что на э́тих плёнках и вы бу́дете говори́ть по-ру́сски.	Learn everything that is on these tapes, and you will speak Russian.

B. The Imperative Mood

The imperative of a verb is formed from the second-person singular present tense. For the singular imperative, replace the ending with -й if the ending is a vowel, with -и if the ending is a consonant (and the first-person singular form of the verb is stressed on the ending), and with -ь if the ending is a consonant (but the first-person singular form is not stressed on the ending). For the plural imperative, add -те to the singular.

Infinitive	Second-Pers. Singular	Familiar, Singular	Plural, Polite
писа́ть to write	пи́ш-ешь	пиши́!	пиши́те!
повторя́ть to repeat	повторя́-ешь	повторя́й!	повторя́йте!
броса́ть to throw	броса́-ешь	броса́й!	броса́йте!
рабо́тать to work	рабо́та-ешь	рабо́тай!	рабо́тайте!
чита́ть to read	чита́-ешь	чита́й!	чита́йте!

The reflexive verb retains its endings: -ся after a consonant or after -й, and -сь after a vowel.

мы́ться to wash (oneself)	мо́-ешься	мо́йся!	мо́йтесь!
занима́ться to study	занима́-ешься	занима́йся!	занима́йтесь!

In giving an order indirectly to a third person, the forms пусть and пуска́й are used with the third-person singular of the verb:

Пусть он чита́ет.	Let him read.	[He should read.]
Пуска́й она́ говорит.	Let her speak.	[She should speak.]

C. Even More on Perfective and Imperfective Verbs

This lesson again shows the use of perfective and imperfective verbs:

Imperfective	Perfective
теря́ть	потеря́ть
находи́ть	найти́

Он потеря́л свой бума́жник.	He lost his wallet (once, this time: perfective).
Она́ ничего́ никогда́ не теря́ет.	She never loses anything (at any time: imperfective).
Я всегда́ что́-нибудь нахожу́.	I always find things (all the time: imperfective).
Сего́дня я нашёл . . .	Today I found (one time, one action: perfective) . . .

D. Word Study

голова́	head
ва́жный	important
вопро́с	question, issue
по́здно	late
де́ло	matter, business
коне́чно	of course
за́втра	tomorrow
ско́ро	soon
да́льше	further

QUIZ 26

1. Я никуда́ не иду́ по́сле обе́да.	a. You may be right.
2. Чья́ газе́та там на столе́?	b. All the best, and have a pleasant trip.
3. Когда́ я хожу́ пешко́м по у́лице, я всегда́ что́-нибудь нахожу́.	c. It's very easy to lose one's way in this city.
4. Как называ́ется э́тот го́род?	d. It is possible to get out of every blind alley by the same road through which you entered.
5. Я потеря́лся и не знал что сказа́ть.	e. Tupik is a situation that has no way out.
6. Как вам не сты́дно, так ско́ро забы́ть меня́!	f. When I came here, I had two hundred thousand rubles.

7. Сего́дня я нашёл о́чень хоро́шую автору́чку.
8. Как я рад, что встре́тил вас!
9. Э́то как раз то, что мне на́до.
10. Э́то гора́здо трудне́е, чем вы ду́маете.
11. Возмо́жно, что вы пра́вы.
12. Мне так жаль того́, кто её потеря́л.
13. Мне ну́жно идти́. Мой по́езд ско́ро отхо́дит.
14. Всего́ хоро́шего и счастли́вого пути́.
15. Я потеря́лся и не знал, куда́ идти́.
16. В э́том го́роде о́чень легко́ заблуди́ться.
17. Из ка́ждого тупика́ мо́жно вы́йти тем же путём, каки́м вы в него́ вошли́.
18. Тупи́к–э́то положе́ние, из кото́рого нет вы́хода.
19. Когда́ я прие́хал сюда́, у меня́ бы́ло две́сти ты́сяч рубле́й.
20. Не ошиба́ется то́лько тот, кто ничего́ не де́лает.

g. I am so sorry for the person who lost it.
h. I lost my way and didn't know where to go.
i. Aren't you ashamed to have forgotten me so soon!
j. I became flustered and didn't know what to say.
k. Whose newspaper is on the table?
l. How glad I am that I met you!
m. I am not going anywhere after dinner.
n. Today I found a very good fountain pen.
o. It's just the thing I need.
p. Only he who does nothing makes no mistakes.
q. What is the name of this city?
r. It's far more difficult than you think.
s. I have to go. My train is leaving soon.
t. When I walk along the street, I always find something.

ANSWERS

1—m; 2—k; 3—t; 4—q; 5—j; 6—i; 7—n; 8—l; 9—o; 10—r; 11—a; 12—g; 13—s; 14—b; 15—h; 16—c; 17—d; 18—e; 19—f; 20—p.

LESSON 38

A. Buying Gifts

О́льга:
Я сего́дня иду́ в магази́н. Мне ну́жно ко́е-что́ купи́ть. Хоти́те пойти́ со мной?

Olga:
I'm going to the store today. I have to buy something. Do you want to go with me?

И́горь:
Мне что́-то не хо́чется, но я ду́маю, что всё же пойду́.

Igor:
I don't feel like it, but I think I'll go anyway.

В како́й магази́н вы хоти́те пойти́?

What store do you want to go to?

О́льга:
Я хочу́ пойти́ в магази́н, кото́рый называ́ется «Де́тский мир». Там есть всё для дете́й любо́го во́зраста.

Olga:
I want to go to a store called "Children's World." There they have everything for children of any age.

И́горь:
Ну, е́сли так, то я пойду́ с ва́ми.

Igor:
Oh, if that's so, then I'll go with you.

О́льга:
Вот и хорошо́. Мне ну́жно купи́ть ю́бку племя́ннице и каку́ю-нибудь игру́шку сы́ну.

Olga:
That's good. I have to buy a skirt for my niece and some sort of toy for my son.

И́горь:
Како́й большо́й магази́н! Как здесь интере́сно.

Igor:
What a big store! How interesting it is here.

О́льга:
Пойдёмте на второ́й эта́ж. Там продаю́т ю́бки.
И́горь:
Вот о́чень краси́вая ю́бка. Вам нра́вится?
О́льга:
Нет, не о́чень. Мне не нра́вится э́тот цвет. Сли́шком я́ркий.
И́горь:
Да что вы! Совсе́м нет! Ведь ва́ша племя́нница така́я молода́я де́вушка.
О́льга:
Да, коне́чно. Но она́ о́чень скро́мная и предпочита́ет что́-нибудь попро́ще. Вот э́та се́рая ю́бка бу́дет лу́чше, пра́вда?
И́горь:
Соверше́нно ве́рно.
О́льга:
Извини́те, ско́лько сто́ит э́та ю́бка?
Продавщи́ца:
Пятьсо́т пятьдеся́т рубле́й. Э́то чи́стая ше́рсть. И о́чень хорошо́ но́сится.
О́льга:
Да? Я её возьму́. Я покупа́ю не для

Olga:
Let's go to the second floor. That's where skirts are sold.
Igor:
There's a very pretty skirt. Do you like it?
Olga:
Not very much. I don't like that color. It's too bright.
Igor:
Oh, what do you mean! No, it's not! [Not at all!] Why, your niece is still so young!
Olga:
Yes, of course. But she is very modest and prefers something simpler. Here, this gray skirt will be better, don't you think?
Igor:
Quite right.
Olga:
Excuse me, how much does this skirt cost?
Salesperson:
Five hundred fifty rubles. It's pure wool. And it wears very well.
Olga:
Yes? I'll take it. I'm not buying it for myself, so

себя́ и е́сли разме́р не подойдёт, мо́жно бу́дет поменя́ть?

if the size isn't right, may I exchange it?

Продавщи́ца:

Коне́чно, в любо́е вре́мя. То́лько не в воскресе́нье. По воскресе́ньям наш магази́н закры́т. Э́то наш выходно́й день.

Salesperson:

Of course. At any time. But not on a Sunday. Our store is closed on Sundays. That's our day off.

И́горь:

А почему́ у них выходно́й день в воскресе́нье?

Igor:

But why do they have their day off on Sunday?

О́льга:

В Росси́и в воскресе́нье все магази́ны закры́ты.

Olga:

In Russia all stores are closed on Sunday.

И́горь:

Вы ещё ничего́ не купи́ли ва́шему сы́ну.

Igor:

You haven't bought anything for your son yet.

О́льга:

Ах да! Вот о́чень хоро́шие ку́бики. Он о́чень лю́бит стро́ить. Ско́лько сто́ят э́ти ку́бики?

Olga:

Oh, yes. Here are some very nice blocks. He loves to build. How much are these blocks?

Продавщи́ца:

Семьсо́т три́дцать рубле́й.

Salesperson:

Seven hundred thirty rubles.

О́льга:

Э́то до́рого, но я всё же их возьму́. Вот ты́сяча три́ста рубле́й.

Olga:

That's a little expensive, but I'll take them anyway. Here are one thousand three hundred rubles.

Продавщи́ца:	*Salesperson:*
Не забу́дьте, пожа́луйста, ва́шу сда́чу.	Don't forget your change, please.
И́горь/О́льга:	*Igor/Olga:*
До свида́ния. Спаси́бо.	Good-bye. Thank you.

B. Use of the Particles To and Нибудь

кто́-то	someone	кто́-нибудь	anyone
где́-то	somewhere	где́-нибудь	anywhere
что́-то	something	что́-нибудь	anything
куда́-то	somewhere	куда́-нибудь	anywhere
почему́-то	for some reason	почему́-нибудь	for any reason

To is used to show that something is known:

Кто́-то пришёл.
Someone came. (I don't know who, but someone did come.)

Он куда́-то пое́дет за́втра.
He is going somewhere tomorrow. (I don't know where, but he does, and it is definite that he is going.)

Нибудь is used to show that nothing is known:

Кто́-нибудь придёт.
Somebody will come. (I don't know who it will be, I don't know if anyone will come, but I think that somebody will come.)

Мне хо́чется куда́-нибудь пое́хать.
I feel like going somewhere. (I don't know where, and I don't know if I will, but I feel like it.)

QUIZ 27

1. Я встаю́ в во́семь часо́в утра́.	a. On Sundays our store is closed.

2. Э́тот биле́т сто́ит шестьсо́т рубле́й.
3. Вы ещё ничего́ не купи́ли ва́шему сы́ну.
4. Покажи́те мне, пожа́луйста, э́ту кни́гу.
5. Мне не нра́вится э́тот цвет. Сли́шком я́ркий.
6. Вот э́та се́рая ю́бка бу́дет лу́чше, пра́вда?
7. По воскресе́ньям наш магази́н закры́т.
8. Э́то до́рого, но я всё же их возьму́.
9. Не забу́дьте, пожа́луйста, ва́шу сда́чу.
10. Мне о́чень нра́вится э́тот го́род.
11. Я всегда́ пью ко́фе с молоко́м.
12. Э́то де́ло вку́са.
13. Како́е вку́сное пиро́жное!
14. Спекта́кль начина́ется без че́тверти во́семь.
15. Он ничего́ не хо́чет де́лать.
16. Она́ была́ в магази́не и ничего́ не купи́ла.
17. Он предпочита́ет что́-нибудь попро́ще.
18. Как ча́сто хо́дят тролле́йбусы?
19. Ка́ждые пять мину́т.
20. Вы не зна́ете, что сего́дня идёт в теа́тре?

b. It's a question of taste.
c. He doesn't want to do anything.
d. He prefers something simpler.
e. The performance starts at a quarter of eight.
f. How often do the buses run?
g. What a delicious pastry!
h. I get up at eight o'clock in the morning.
i. She was in the store and didn't buy anything.
j. Every five minutes.
k. This ticket costs six hundred rubles.
l. You haven't bought anything for your son yet.
m. Do you know what is playing at the theatre today?
n. I don't like that color. It's too bright.
o. That's expensive, but I'll take them anyway.
p. I like this city very much.
q. Here, this gray skirt will be better, don't you think [isn't it true]?
r. I always drink coffee with milk.
s. Don't forget your change, please.
t. Please, show me this book.

ANSWERS

1—h; 2—k; 3—l; 4—t; 5—n; 6—q; 7—a; 8—o; 9—s; 10—p; 11—r; 12—b; 13—g; 14—e; 15—c; 16—i; 17—d; 18—f; 19—j; 20—m.

LESSON 39

A. Two Colleagues

Илья́:
Здра́вствуйте, ми́лая Наде́жда Гео́ргиевна!

Ilya:
Hello, dear Nadezhda Georgievna!

Наде́жда:
Здра́вствуйте, Илья́ Петро́вич! Как я ра́да вас ви́деть! Я как раз собира́лась вам позвони́ть.

Nadezhda:
How are you, Ilya Petrovich! I am so happy to see you. I was just about to call you.

Илья́:
А что тако́е?

Ilya:
What's the matter?

Наде́жда:
У меня́ в суббо́ту бу́дет приём. Приезжа́ет гру́ппа коммерса́нтов из Росси́и. С не́которыми из них вы уже знако́мы по рабо́те в ба́нке. По́мните Васи́лия Смирно́ва и Никола́я Радзи́нского?

Nadezhda:
I am having a reception on Saturday. A group of businessmen from Russia is coming. Some of them you already know through your work at the bank. Do you remember Vasily Smirnov and Nikolai Radzinsky?

Илья́:
Да, да, коне́чно. Как я могу́ вам помо́чь?

Ilya:
Yes, yes, of course. How can I help you?

Наде́жда:
Да́же нело́вко проси́ть. Де́ло в том, что Джим, мой муж,

Nadezhda:
It's awkward to even ask. The thing is that Jim, my husband, is

заинтересо́ван в организа́ции совме́стного предприя́тия в Оде́ссе. Но нужна́ подде́ржка ме́стных власте́й. Тепе́рь, коне́чно, Украи́на незави́сима и поэ́тому всё осложнено́. Кро́ме того́, Джим о́чень пло́хо говори́т по-ру́сски. Коро́че, нужны́ перево́дчики. Я, коне́чно, сама́ бу́ду переводи́ть, но гру́ппа больша́я. В о́бщем, са́ми понима́ете.

interested in organizing a joint venture in Odessa. But the support of local authorities is what is needed. Now, of course, the Ukraine is independent, and everything is complicated. Besides, Jim's Russian is very bad. In short we need interpreters. I will certainly interpret myself, but the group is large. Well, you understand.

Илья́:

Наде́жда Гео́ргиевна! О чём речь! Вы же зна́ете, что я всегда́ гото́в помо́чь. Да, к тому́ же, я сам хоте́л переговори́ть с Радзи́нским насчёт капиталовложе́ний в ру́сские компа́ние.

Ilya:

Nadezhda Georgievna! What are you talking about! You know that I am always ready to help. Besides, I wantedto have a chat with Radzinsky myself about investments in Russian companies.

Наде́жда:

Ну и сла́ва Бо́гу! В о́бщем, жду́ вас у себя́ в 7 часо́в. Я заказа́ла пирожки́,

Nadezhda:

Thank God! So I am expecting you at my place at seven o'clock. I ordered meat pies,

икру́ и, коне́чно, я́щик шампа́нского и ру́сскую во́дку.	caviar, and, of course, a case of champagne and Russian vodka.
Илья́:	*Ilya:*
Пока́ перевожу́, придётся без во́дки обойти́сь.	I will have to do without vodka while interpreting.
Наде́жда:	*Nadezhda:*
Коне́чно, коне́чно. Огро́мное спаси́бо. Жду.	Of course, of course. I am very grateful. I'm expecting you.

B. At The Museum

I. Nina asks the way to the Hermitage:

Ни́на: **Извини́те, пожа́луйста. Как дойти́ до Эрмита́жа?**
Nina: Excuse me, how can I get to the Hermitage?

Прохо́жий: **Да э́то недалеко́ отсю́да. Иди́те пря́мо, и музе́й бу́дет сле́ва от вас.**
Passer-by: It's not far from here. Go straight ahead, and the museum will be on the left.

Ни́на: **Спаси́бо. Мо́жно дойти́ пешко́м?**
Nina: Thanks. So I can walk there?

Прохо́жий: **Да, коне́чно! Жела́ю вам прия́тно провести́ вре́мя в Петербу́рге.**
Passer-by: Yes, of course! Have a pleasant stay in St. Petersburg.

II. Nina goes to the Hermitage with her friend Ivan:

Ни́на: **Зна́ете, я о́чень интересу́юсь ру́сским иску́сством.**
Nina: You know, I'm very interested in Russian art.

Ива́н: **Я то́же! Я интересу́юсь анти́чным и средневеко́вым иску́сством.**
Ivan: Me too! I'm interested in ancient and medieval art.

Како́й ваш люби́мый пери́од?
What period do you like the best?

Ни́на: **Я обожа́ю передви́жников! Смотри́те! Вот карти́на худо́жника-передви́жника. Кто её написа́л?**
Nina: I love the Wanderers (*the Peredvizhniki*)! Look! There's a picture by one of the Wandering painters! Who painted it?

Ива́н: **Э́то карти́на Ре́пина.**
Ivan: That's by Repin.

Ни́на: **Да, ве́рно. В како́м году́ он её написа́л?**
Nina: Oh, yes. What year did he complete it?

Ива́н: **Одну́ мину́точку. Я посмотрю́ . . . В ты́сяча восемьсо́т во́семьдесят четвёртом году́.**
Ivan: Just a moment. I'll look . . . in 1884.

LESSON 40

A. Problems of the Planet

Пробле́мы плане́ты.

Необдума́нные индустриа́льные прое́кты ча́сто веду́т к наруше́нию экологи́ческого бала́нса на земле́. Поэ́тому за после́дние не́сколько лет всё бо́льше люде́й в ми́ре начина́ют выступа́ть за охра́ну приро́ды.

Большу́ю трево́гу вызыва́ет потепле́ние кли́мата. Учёные пока́ не мо́гут назва́ть то́чной причи́ны потепле́ния земно́го кли́мата. Мо́жет быть э́то свя́зано с разруше́нием озо́нового сло́я атмосфе́ры. Э́то происхо́дит, когда́ фрео́ны и други́е синтети́ческие вещества́, содержа́щие хлор, поступа́ют в атмосфе́ру.

Ру́сские специали́сты нашли́ заме́ну фрео́ну: соедине́ние пропа́на и бута́на, безвре́дное для атмосфе́рного сло́я. Кро́ме того́, плани́руется по́лное прекраще́ние вы́пуска фрео́нов росси́йской хими́ческой промы́шленностью. Росси́я принима́ет серьёзные ме́ры для разреше́ния пробле́мы разру́шения озо́нового сло́я.

Обы́чные лю́ди то́же мо́гут помо́чь в э́том де́ле. Для э́того ну́жно прекрати́ть по́льзоваться косме́тикой, в кото́рой распыли́телем слу́жат фрео́ны, ре́же включа́ть кондиционе́р, и покупа́ть ка́чественные холоди́льники. Мы все должны́ уча́ствовать в охра́не приро́ды.

Thoughtless industrial projects often lead to the disturbance of the ecological balance on earth. Therefore, in recent years, more and more people in the world have begun to speak out in support of protecting nature.

Warming of the climate (global warming) causes great alarm. Scientists cannot yet name the exact reason for the warming of the earth's climate. Perhaps it is related to the destruction of the ozone layer in the atmosphere. This happens when Freons and other synthetic compounds containing chlorine enter the atmosphere.

Russian specialists found a substitute for Freons—a compound of propane and butane, which is harmless to the atmospheric layer. Moreover, a complete halt in the production of Freons by the Russian chemical industry is being planned. Russia is taking serious measures to solve the problem of the destruction of the ozone layer.

Ordinary people can also help in this matter. For example, it is necessary to stop using cosmetic products in which Freons are propellants, to turn air-conditioning on less often, and to buy refrigerators of good quality. We should all participate in the protection of nature.

B. Participles and Gerunds

Participles and gerunds are very important parts of the Russian language, so it is necessary to know how to recognize and to understand them. However, it should be made clear that they are not used very much in simple conversation, but rather in literature and scientific writing.

Participles are verbal adjectives; gerunds are verbal adverbs. Participles are adjectives made out of verbs. The difference between an adjective and a participle is that a participle retains the verbal qualities of tense, aspect, and voice. In every other respect they are adjectives. They have three genders: masculine, feminine, and neuter. They decline like adjectives and agree with the words they modify in gender, case, and number.

	PRESENT PARTICIPLE	PAST PARTICIPLE
говори́ть	говоря́щий, -ая, -ее, -ие	говори́вший, -ая -ее, -ие

PREPOSITIONAL PLURAL:

Мы говори́м о говоря́щих по-англи́йски ученика́х.
We are talking about students who speak English.

Gerunds are verbal adverbs and as such do not change, but have present and past tenses. The present tense is formed from the imperfective; the past tense must be formed from the perfective. The present tense is characterized by two actions at the same time. In the past tense there are two actions, one following the other; when the first action is completed, the second one starts.

PRESENT TENSE:

чита́ть

Чита́я, он улыба́лся.
While reading, he was smiling. (The two actions are simultaneous.)

PAST TENSE:

прочита́ть

Прочита́в газе́ту, он встал и ушёл.
Having finished reading the paper, he got up and went away. (One action follows the other.)

FINAL REVIEW

1. Я хочу́ хорошо́ _____ по-ру́сски. I want to speak Russian well.
2. Кто _____ э́то? Who said that?
3. _____ вы хоти́те ви́деть? Whom do you wish to see?
4. _____ вы да́ли мою́ кни́гу? Whom did you give my book to?
5. С _____ вы бы́ли в теа́тре вчера́? Whom were you with in the theatre yesterday?
6. Э́то всё, _____ он сказа́л. That's all that he said.
7. Для _____ э́то? What's this for?
8. На _____ вы сиди́те? What are you sitting on?
9. У _____ нет карандаша́. I don't have a pencil.
10. О _____ вы говори́ли? Whom were you talking about?
11. У _____ есть ка́рта Москвы́? Do you have a map of Moscow?
12. Вот _____ магази́н. Here's a good store.
13. Я _____ пить. I want a [to] drink.
14. У _____ есть всё. They have everything.
15. _____ удивля́етесь? What are you surprised at?
16. У _____ нет бра́та. She has no brother.
17. Мне _____ пить. I'm thirsty. [I feel like drinking.]
18. Я _____ по-ру́сски. I speak Russian.
19. Мы _____ чита́ть. We want to read.
20. Они́ _____ хорошо́. They understand well.
21. Вы говори́те сли́шком _____. You speak too fast.
22. Пожа́луйста, говори́те _____. Please speak slower.
23. _____ я понима́ю. Now I understand.
24. _____ вре́мени? What time is it?
25. Он _____ домо́й. He goes home (on foot).
26. Мы _____ обе́дать до́ма. We will have dinner at home.
27. Как вас _____ ? What is your name?
28. Как _____ э́тот го́род? What is the name of this city?
29. Спаси́бо, я _____ не хочу́. Thank you, I don't want any more.
30. _____ сего́дня число́? What is today's date?
31. Мне о́чень _____ э́та книга. I like this book very much.
32. Он _____ весь ве́чер. He spoke all evening.
33. Он _____ всё, что он знал. He said all he knew (perfective).
34. У меня́ до́ма мно́го _____. I have a lot of books at home.

35. Я хочу́ _____ молока́. I want some more milk.
36. За́втра я _____ письмо́ бра́ту. Tomorrow I will write a letter to my brother.
37. _____ она́ краси́вая! How pretty she is!
38. Он встаёт _____ ка́ждый день. He gets up early every day.
39. Она́ _____ в Москве́. She lived in Moscow.
40. Де́ти _____ по-ру́сски. The children will speak Russian (imperfective).
41. Вчера́ мы чита́ли _____. We read the paper yesterday.
42. _____ ему́, что я бу́ду у него́ до́ма за́втра. Tell him that I will be at his house tomorrow.
43. _____ войти́? May I come in?
44. Он взял кни́гу и _____ . He took the book and left.
45. Он всегда́ всё _____ . He always forgets everything.
46. Здесь _____ кури́ть. No smoking here.
47. Он ничего́ _____ . He knows nothing. [He doesn't know anything.]
48. Он никогда́ _____ в Москве́. He has never been to Moscow.
49. До́ктор сказа́л, что вам _____ кури́ть. The doctor said that you can't smoke.
50. Всё _____ , что _____ конча́ется. All's well that ends well.
51. Я иду́ на _____ . I am going to work.
52. Мой брат рабо́тает _____ . My brother works at home.
53. Мы живём в _____ . We live in town.
54. Он пи́шет _____ . He is writing with a pencil.
55. Я смотрю́ на _____ . I am looking at my brother.
56. Он лю́бит чита́ть _____ . He likes to read newspapers.
57. У меня́ нет _____ _____ . I don't have black pencils.
58. Мы говори́м о моём _____ . We are talking about my friend.
59. У него́ нет _____ . He has no sister.
60. Он пи́шет письмо́ _____ . He is writing a letter to his wife.

ANSWERS

1. говори́ть
2. сказа́л
3. Кого́
4. Кому́
5. кем
6. что
7. чего́
8. чём
9. меня́
10. ком
11. вас
12. хоро́ший
13. хочу́
14. них
15. Чему́
16. неё
17. хо́чется
18. говорю́
19. хоти́м
20. понима́ют
21. бы́стро
22. ме́дленнее
23. Тепе́рь
24. Ско́лько
25. идёт
26. бу́дем
27. зову́т
28. называ́ется
29. бо́льше
30. Како́е
31. нра́вится
32. говори́л
33. сказа́л
34. книг
35. ещё
36. напишу́
37. Кака́я
38. ра́но
39. жила́
40. бу́дут говори́ть
41. газе́ту
42. Скажи́те
43. Мо́жно
44. ушёл
45. забыва́ет
46. нельзя́
47. не зна́ет
48. не был
49. нельзя́
50. хорошо́ хорошо́
51. рабо́ту
52. до́ма
53. го́роде
54. карандашо́м
55. бра́та
56. газе́ты
57. чёрных карандаше́й
58. дру́ге
59. сестры́
60. жене́

SUMMARY OF RUSSIAN GRAMMAR

1. The Russian Alphabet

RUSSIAN LETTER	SCRIPT		NAME
Аа	*А*	*а*	ah
Бб	*Б*	*б*	beh
Вв	*В*	*в*	veh
Гг	*Г*	*г*	geh
Дд	*Д*	*д*	deh
Ее	*Е*	*е*	yeh
Ёё	*Ё*	*ё*	yoh
Жж	*Ж*	*ж*	zheh
Зз	*З*	*з*	zeh
Ии	*И*	*и*	ee
Йй	*Й*	*й*	ee (i short)
Кк	*К*	*к*	kah
Лл	*Л*	*л*	ell
Мм	*М*	*м*	em
Нн	*Н*	*н*	en
Оо	*О*	*о*	oh
Пп	*П*	*п*	peh
Рр	*Р*	*р*	err
Сс	*С*	*с*	ess
Тт	*Т*	*т*	teh
Уу	*У*	*у*	ooh
Фф	*Ф*	*ф*	eff
Хх	*Х*	*х*	khah
Цц	*Ц*	*ц*	tseh
Чч	*Ч*	*ч*	cheh
Шш	*Ш*	*ш*	shah
Щщ	*Щ*	*щ*	shchah
Ыы	*Ы*	*ы*	yerih

Ьь	*ь*	*ь*	soft sign
Ъъ	*ъ*	*ъ*	hard sign
Ээ	*Э*	*э*	eh
Юю	*Ю*	*ю*	yoo
Яя	*Я*	*я*	yah

2. Pronunciation

VOWELS

The letter а, when stressed, is pronounced like the English *ah;* when unstressed before a stressed syllable, а is pronounced *ah,* but shorter, and in most other positions is given a neuter sound.

The letter о, when stressed, is pronounced like the English *oh;* when unstressed in first place before the stressed syllable or used initially, о is pronounced *ah,* and in all other positions has a neuter sound.

The letter у is pronounced both stressed and unstressed like the English *ooh.*

The letter ы is pronounced somewhat like the *iy* sound in *buoy.*

The letter э is pronounced like the *eh* in *echo.*

Five vowels—е, ё, и, ю, я—have a glide (the sound similar to the final sound in the English word "may") in front of them. The function of these vowels is the palatalization of the preceding consonant, to which they lose the above-mentioned glide. However, when they follow a vowel or a soft or hard sign, or when they appear in the initial position of a word, they are pronounced as in the alphabet—i.e., with an initial glide.

The letter и always palatalizes the preceding consonant and is pronounced like the *ee* in *beet,* except when it follows the letters ж, ц, ш, which are never palatalized, when it is pronounced like the Russian sound ы.

The letter й is never stressed. It is pronounced like the final sound in *boy.*

The letter е always palatalizes the consonant that precedes it, except when that consonant is ж, ц, ш. When stressed, it is pronounced like the *yeh* in *yet;* in unstressed positions it is pronounced like the *eh* in *bet.* Initially, it is pronounced with the glide: stressed, like *yeh;* unstressed, like *yeeh.*

The letter ё always palatalizes the preceding consonant, and is always stressed. It is pronounced like the *yo* in *yoke.*

The letter я always palatalizes the preceding consonant; when stressed, it is pronounced *yah;* when unstressed, it is pronounced like a shortened *ee.* Initially, it retains its glide; when stressed, it is pronounced *yah,* unstressed, yeeh.

The letter ю always palatalizes the preceding consonant. It is pronounced *ooh* in the body of the word; initially it retains its glide and is pronounced *yooh.*

The letter ь is called the "soft" sign; it palatalizes the preceding consonant, allowing the following vowel to retain its glide.

The letter ъ is called the "hard" sign. It indicates that the preceding consonant remains hard and that the following vowel retains its glide.

Consonants

As in every language, Russian consonants may be voiced or voiceless. The pairs are:

RUSSIAN	ENGLISH	
б в г д ж з	(voiced)	b v g d zh z
п ф к т ш с	(voiceless)	p f k t sh s

When two consonants are pronounced together,

they must both be either voiced or voiceless. In Russian, the second one always remains as it is, and the first one changes accordingly:

всё, все, вчера́; в = v; pronounced *f*

сде́лать, сдать; с = s; pronounced *z*

The preposition в (in) is very often pronounced *f:*

в шко́ле is pronouned *fshkoh - leh.*

All consonants are voiceless at the end of a word. All consonants can also be hard or soft (i.e., palatalized or nonpalatalized) when followed by the letters, е, ё, и, ю, я or ь. Only the consonants ж, ц, and ш are always hard.

3. Gender

All Russian nouns, pronouns, adjectives, and ordinal numerals, as well as cardinal numerals and even several verb forms have gender: masculine, feminine, or neuter. In the plural there is only one form for all genders.

Masculine	Feminine	Neuter	Plural
Most nouns and pronouns and the past tense of verbs end in:			
hard consonant	а, я	о, е	а, ы, и
Most adjectives, ordinal numerals, and participles end in:			
ой, ый, ий	ая, яя	ое, ее	ые, ие

NOTE
Pronouns, adjectives, and ordinal numerals always agree in gender with the nouns they modify or represent.

4. Cases

a. With few exceptions, all nouns, pronouns, and adjectives decline. Each declension has six cases:

Nominative:	Кто? Что?	Who? What?
Genitive:	Кого́? Чего́?	Whom? What?
	От кого́? От чего́?	From whom? From what?
	У кого́? У чего́?	At or by whom/what?
	Без кого́? Без чего́?	Without whom/what?
Dative:	Кому́? Чему́?	To whom? To what?
	К кому́? К чему́?	Toward whom/what?
Accusative:	Кого́? Что?	Whom? What?
	Куда́?	Where (direction toward)?
Instrumental:	Кем? Чем?	By whom? By what?
	С кем? С чем?	With whom? With what?
Prepositional	О ком? О чём?	About whom/what?
or Locative:	В ком? В чём?	In whom? In what?
	Где?	Where (location)?

b. Overall characteristics of the cases and most used prepositions:

1. The nominative case supplies the subject of the sentence.

2. The genitive case is the case of possession and negation. It is also used with many prepositions, the most common of which are:

без	without
для	for
до	up to
из	out of
о́коло	near

от	from
по́сле	after
у	at or by

3. The dative case is used in the meaning of "to whom." Prepositions governing the dative case are:

к	to
по	along

4. The accusative is the direct object case. Prepositions used with this case include:

в	to, into
за	behind (direction)
на	to, into, on (direction)

5. The instrumental case indicates the manner of action or instrument with which the action is performed. Prepositions governing the instrumental case include:

ме́жду	between
пе́ред	in front of
над	over
под	under (location)
за	behind (location)

6. The prepositional or locative case indicates location and is also used when speaking about something or someone. The prepositions most frequently used with this case are:

в	in
на	on
о	about
при	in the presence of

5. Declension of Nouns

	Masculine Singular			
	Hard		Soft	
	Animate	Inanimate	Animate	Inanimate
	student	question	inhabitant	shed
Nom.	студе́нт	вопро́с	жи́тель	сара́й
Gen.	студе́нт-а	вопро́с-а	жи́тел-я	сара́-я
Dat.	студе́нт-у	вопро́с-у	жи́тел-ю	сара́-ю
Acc.	студе́нт-а	вопро́с	жи́тел-я	сара́й
Inst.	студе́нт-ом	вопро́с-ом	жи́тел-ем	сара́-ем
Prep.	о студе́нт-е	о вопро́с-е	о жи́тел-е	о сара́-е

	Masculine Plural			
Nom.	студе́нт-ы	вопро́с-ы	жи́тел-и	сара́-и
Gen.	студе́нт-ов	вопро́с-ов	жи́тел-ей	сара́-ев
Dat.	студе́нт-ам	вопро́с-ам	жи́тел-ям	сара́-ям
Acc.	студе́нт-ов	вопро́с-ы	жи́тел-ей	сара́-и
Inst.	студе́нт-ами	вопро́с-ами	жи́тел-ями	сара́-ями
Prep.	о студе́нт-ах	о вопро́с-ах	о жи́тел-ях	о сара́-ях

NOTE

The accusative case of animate masculine nouns is the same as the genitive, while the accusative of inanimate masculine nouns is the same as the nominative.

	Feminine Singular		
	Hard	Soft	
	room	earth	family
Nom.	ко́мната	земля́	семья́
Gen.	ко́мнат-ы	земл-и́	семь-и́
Dat.	ко́мнат-е	земл-е́	семь-е́
Acc.	ко́мнат-у	зе́мл-ю	семь-ю́
Inst.	ко́мнат-ой(-ою)	земл-ёй(-ёю)	семь-ёй(-ёю)
Prep.	о ко́мнат-е	о земл-е́	о семь-е́

	Feminine Plural		
Nom.	ко́мнат-ы	зе́мл-и	се́мь-и
Gen.	ко́мнат	земе́л-ь	сем-е́й
Dat.	ко́мнат-ам	зе́мл-ям	се́мь-ям
Acc.	ко́мнат-ы	зе́мл-и	се́мь-и
Inst.	ко́мнат-ами	зе́мл-ями	се́мь-ями
Prep.	о ко́мнат-ах	о зе́мл-ях	о се́мь-ях

	Neuter Singular		
	Hard	Soft	
	window	sea	wish
Nom.	окно́	мо́ре	жела́ние
Gen.	окн-а́	мо́р-я	жела́н-ия
Dat.	окн-у́	мо́р-ю	жела́н-ию
Acc.	окн-о́	мо́р-е	жела́н-ие
Inst.	окн-о́м	мо́р-ем	жела́н-ием
Prep.	об[1] окн-е́	о мо́р-е	о жела́н-ии

	Neuter Plural		
Nom.	о́кн-а	мор-я́	жела́н-ия
Gen.	о́к-он	мор-е́й	жела́н-ий
Dat.	о́кн-ам	мор-я́м	жела́н-иям
Acc.	о́кн-а	мор-я́	жела́н-ия
Inst.	о́кн-ами	мор-я́ми	жела́н-иями
Prep.	об[1] о́кн-ах	о мор-я́х	о жела́н-иях

[1] **б** is added to the preposition here for the sake of euphony.

Some Irregular Declensions

	Singular				
	Masc.	Feminine		Neuter	
	ROAD	MOTHER	DAUGHTER	NAME	CHILD
Nom.	путь	мать	дочь	и́мя	дитя́
Gen.	пут-и́	ма́т-ери	до́ч-ери	и́м-ени	дит-я́ти[1]
Dat.	пут-и́	ма́т-ери	до́ч-ери	и́м-ени	дит-я́ти[1]
Acc.	путь	ма́ть	до́чь	и́мя	дитя́
Inst.	пут-ём	ма́т-ерью	до́ч-ерью	и́м-енем	дит-я́тей[1]
Prep.	о пут-и́	о ма́т-ери	о до́ч-ери	об и́м-ени	о дит-я́ти[1]

	Plural				
Nom.	пут-и́	ма́т-ери	до́ч-ери	им-ена́	де́т-и
Gen.	пут-е́й	мат-ере́й	доч-ере́й	им-ён	дет-е́й
Dat.	пут-я́м	мат-еря́м	доч-еря́м	им-ена́м	де́т-ям
Acc.	пут-и́	мат-ере́й[2]	доч-ере́й	им-ена́	дет-е́й[2]
Inst.	пут-я́ми	мат-еря́ми	доч-еря́ми	им-ена́ми	дет-ьми́
Prep.	о пут-я́х	о мат-еря́х	о доч-еря́х	об им-ена́х	о де́т-ях

6. Declension of Adjectives

	Singular					
	Masc.	Fem.	Neut.	Masc.	Fem.	Neut.
	ый	ая	ое	ой	ая	ое
Nom.	но́вый	но́вая	но́вое	сухо́й	суха́я	сухо́е
Gen.	но́в-ого	но́в-ой	но́в-ого	сух-о́го	сух-о́й	сух-о́го
Dat.	но́в-ому	но́в-ой	но́в-ому	сух-о́му	сух-о́й	сух-о́му
Acc.	Same as nom. or gen.	но́в-ую	но́в-ое	Same as nom. or gen.	сух-у́ю	сух-о́е
Inst.	но́в-ым	но́в-ой(-ою)	но́в-ым	сух-и́м	сух-о́й(-ою)	сух-и́м
Prep.	о но́в-ом	о но́в-ой	о но́в-ом	о сух-о́м	о сухо́й	о сух-о́м

[1] Old form seldom used.

[2] The accusative plural of animate neuter nouns and most feminine nouns is the same as the genitive plural.

	Plural	
Nom.	но́в-ые	сух-и́е
Gen.	но́в-ых	сух-и́х
Dat.	но́в-ым	сух-и́м
Acc.	Same as nom. or gen.	Same as nom. or gen.
Inst.	но́в-ыми	сух-и́ми
Prep.	о но́в-ых	о сух-и́х

	Singular			Plural
	Masc.	Fem.	Neut.	
Nom.	си́н-ий	си́н-яя	си́н-ее	си́н-ие
Gen.	си́н-его	си́н-ей	си́н-его	си́н-их
Dat.	си́н-ему	си́н-ей	си́н-ему	си́н-им
Acc.	Same as nom. or gen.	си́н-юю	си́н-ее	Same as nom. or gen.
Inst.	си́н-им	си́н-ей(-ею)	си́н-им	си́н-ими
Prep.	о си́н-ем	о си́н-ей	о си́н-ем	о си́н-их

7. Declension of Pronouns

	Singular				
	1st Person	2nd Person	3rd Person		
			Masc.	Neut.	Fem.
Nom.	я	ты	он	оно́	она́
Gen.	меня́	тебя́	его́	его́	её
Dat.	мне́	тебе́	ему́	ему́	ей
Acc.	меня́	тебя́	его́	его́	её
Instr.	мной(-о́ю)	тобо́й(-о́ю)	им	им	ей, е́ю
Prep.	обо мне́	о тебе́	о нём	о нём	о ней

	Plural		
	1st Person	2nd Person	3rd Person
Nom.	мы	вы	они́
Gen.	нас	вас	их
Dat.	нам	вам	им
Acc.	нас	вас	их
Instr.	на́ми	ва́ми	и́ми
Prep.	о нас	о вас	о них

Reflexive Pronoun
Sing. or Plural
—
себя́
себе́
себя́
собо́й(-о́ю)
о себе́

	my			
	Singular			Plural
	Masc.	Fem.	Neuter	All genders
Nom.	мой	моя́	моё	мои́
Gen.	моего́	мое́й	моего́	мои́х
Dat.	моему́	мое́й	моему́	мои́м
Acc.	Same as nom. or gen.	мою́	моё	Same as nom. or gen.
Inst.	мои́м	мое́й(-е́ю)	мои́м	мои́ми
Prep.	о моём	о мое́й	о моём	о мои́х

твой (your, sing.), свой (one's own, their own) are declined in the same way.

For the third-person possessive, the genitive case of the personal pronouns is used. It always agrees with the gender and number of the possessor.

Nominative	Genitive	
он	его́	his
она́	её	her
оно́	его́	its
они́	их	their

	Our			
	Singular			Plural
	Masc.	Fem.	Neut.	All genders
Nom.	наш	на́ша	на́ше	на́ши
Gen.	на́ш-его	на́ш-ей	на́ш-его	на́ш-их
Dat.	на́ш-ему	на́ш-ей	на́ш-ему	на́ш-им
Acc.	Same as nom or or gen.	на́ш-у	на́ше	Same as nom. or gen.
Inst.	на́ш-им	на́ш-ей(-ею)	на́ш-им	на́ш-ими
Prep.	о на́ш-ем	о на́ш-ей	о на́ш-ем	о на́ш-их

ваш (your, *plural* or *polite*) is declined in the same way.

	All			
	Singular			Plural
	Masc.	Fem.	Neut.	All genders
Nom.	весь	вся	всё	все
Gen.	вс-его́	вс-ей	вс-его́	вс-ех
Dat.	вс-ему́	вс-ей	вс-ему́	вс-ем
Acc.	Same as nom. or gen.	вс-ю	всё	Same as nom. or gen.
Inst.	вс-ем	вс-ей(-ею)	вс-ем	вс-е́ми
Prep.	обо вс-ём	обо вс-ей	обо вс-ём	обо вс-ех

	Singular this			Plural these
	Masc.	Fem.	Neut.	All genders
Nom.	э́тот	э́та	э́то	э́ти
Gen.	э́т-ого	э́т-ой	э́т-ого	э́т-их
Dat.	э́т-ому	э́т-ой	э́т-ому	э́т-им
Acc.	Same as nom. or gen.	э́т-у	э́то	Same as nom. or gen.
Inst.	э́т-им	э́т-ой	э́т-им	э́т-ими
Prep.	об э́т-ом	об э́т-ой	об э́т-ом	об э́т-их

	Singular that			Plural those
	Masc.	Fem.	Neut.	All genders
Nom.	тот	та	та	те
Gen.	т-ого́	т-ой	т-ого́	т-ех
Dat.	т-ому́	т-ой	т-ому́	т-ем
Acc.	Same as nom. or gen.	т-у	т-о	Same as nom. or gen.
Inst.	т-ем	т-ой	т-ем	т-е́ми
Prep.	о т-ом	о т-ой	о т-ом	о т-ех

	Singular oneself			Plural themselves
	Masc.	Fem.	Neut.	All genders
Nom.	сам	сама́	само́	са́ми
Gen.	сам-ого́	сам-о́й	сам-ого́	сам-и́х
Dat.	сам-ому́	сам-о́й	сам-ому́	сам-и́м
Acc.	Same as nom. or gen.	сам-у́	сам-о́	Same as nom. or gen.
Inst.	сам-и́м	сам-о́й	сам-и́м	сам-и́ми
Prep.	о сам-о́м	о сам-о́й	о сам-о́м	о сам-и́х

	Singular whose			Plural
	Masc.	Fem.	Neut.	All genders
Nom.	чей	чья	чьё	чьи
Gen.	чьего́	чьей	чьего́	чьих
Dat.	чьему́	чьей	чьему́	чьим
Acc.	Same as nom. or gen.	чью	чьё	Same as nom. or gen.
Inst.	чьим	чьей	чьим	чьи́ми
Prep.	о чьём	о чьей	о чьём	о чьих

8. Comparative of Adjectives

To form the comparative of an adjective, drop the gender ending and add -ее for all genders and the plural, as well. The adjective does not decline in the comparative:

краси́вый	pretty
краси́в-ее	prettier
тёплый	warm
тепл-е́е	warmer
весёлый	merry
весел-е́е	merrier

Irregular Comparative Forms

хоро́ший	good
лу́чше	better
большо́й	big
бо́льше	bigger
ма́ленький	small
ме́ньше	smaller
широ́кий	wide
ши́ре	wider
у́зкий	narrow
у́же	narrower
плохо́й	bad
ху́же	worse
высо́кий	tall
вы́ше	taller
ти́хий	quiet
ти́ше	quieter
дорого́й	dear/expensive
доро́же	dearer/more expensive
просто́й	simple
про́ще	simpler

то́лстый	fat
то́лще	fatter

9. Superlative of Adjectives

The superlative of adjectives has two forms. The simpler form—the one we will discuss here—makes use of the word са́мый, са́мая, са́мое, са́мые (the most):

са́мый большо́й	the biggest
са́мая краси́вая	the prettiest
са́мый у́мный	the most clever

The word са́мый declines with the adjective:

в са́мом большо́м до́ме
in the very largest house

Он пришёл с са́мой краси́вой же́нщиной.
He came with the prettiest woman.

10. Cases Used with Cardinal Numerals

оди́н (*m.*), одна́ (*f.*), одно́ (*n.*), одни́ (*pl.*)
два (*m.*), две (*f.*), два (*n.*)

A. When the number is used in the nominative case:

after оди́н, одна́, одно́—use the nominative *singular.*
after одни́—use the nominative *plural.*
after два, две, три, четы́ре—use the genitive *singular.*
after пять, шесть, семь, etc.—use the genitive *plural.*

B. When the number is compound, the case of the noun depends on the last digit:

два́дцать оди́н каранда́ш (nominative *singular*)
twenty-one pencils
два́дцать два карандаша́ (genitive *singular*)
twenty-two pencils
два́дцать пять карандаше́й (genitive *plural*)
twenty-five pencils

11. Declension of Cardinal Numerals

All cardinal numerals decline, agreeing in case with the noun they modify (with the exception of the nominative case, discussed above).

Я оста́лся без одно́й копе́йки. (genitive *singular*)
I was left without one cent.

Он был там оди́н ме́сяц без двух дней. (genitive *plural*)
He was there one month less two days.

Мы пришли́ к пяти́ часа́м. (dative *plural*)
We arrived about five o'clock.

Они́ говоря́т о семи́ челове́ках. (prepositional *plural*)
They are speaking about seven people.

Declension of Numerals

	Singular one			Plural only
	Masc.	Fem.	Neut.	(all genders)
Nom.	оди́н	одна́	одно́	одни́
Gen.	одного́	одно́й	одного́	одни́х
Dat.	одному́	одно́й	одному́	одни́м
Acc.	Same as nom. or gen.	одну́	одно́	Same as nom. or gen.
Inst.	одни́м	одно́й(-о́ю)	одни́м	одни́ми
Prep.	об одно́м	об одно́й	об одно́м	об одни́х

	two	three	four	five
Nom.	два, две	три	четы́ре	пять
Gen.	двух	трёх	четырёх	пяти́
Dat.	двум	трём	четырём	пяти́
Acc.	Same as nom. or gen.	Same as nom. or gen.	Same as nom. or gen.	пять
Inst.	двумя́	тремя́	четырьмя́	пятью́
Prep.	о двух	о трёх	о четырёх	о пяти́

NOTE
All numbers from 6 to 20 follow the same declension pattern as 5.

12. Ordinal Numerals

All ordinal numerals are like adjectives, and decline in the same way as adjectives:

Masc.	Fem.	Neut.	Plural (all genders)
пе́рвый второ́й	пе́рвая втора́я	пе́рвое второ́е	пе́рвые вторы́е

When they are compound, only the last digit changes its form, and only that digit is declined.

двадца́тый век	twentieth century
Э́то бы́ло три́дцать пе́рвого декабря́.	That was on December 31.
тре́тий раз	third time
Втора́я мирова́я война́ ко́нчилась в ты́сяча девятьсо́т со́рок пя́том году́.	The Second World War ended in 1945 (one thousand, nine hundred, forty-fifth year).

пя́тый год	
(в) пя́том году́	(prepositional singular)

13. Double Negatives

With words such as:

ничего́	nothing
никто́	nobody
никогда́	never
никуда́	nowhere

a second negative must be used:

I nothing	don't	(verb)
Я ничего́	не	хочу́, зна́ю.
Nobody	don't	(verb)
Никто́	не	ви́дит, говори́т.
Never	don't	(verb)
Он никогда́	не	был в Москве́.
Мы никогда́	не	говори́м по-ру́сски.

A negative adverb or pronoun must use a negative with the verb it modifies. (For more on negative expressions, see pages 97–98.)

14. Verbs

Russian verbs have two conjugations. Infinitives of most verbs belonging to the first conjugation end with -ать or -ять. Infinitives of verbs belonging to the second conjugation end with -еть or -ить. Although this is true of a great body of Russian verbs, there are many exceptions, several of which are included in this summary.

A. Typical Conjugations of Imperfective Verbs:

FIRST CONJUGATION
чита́ть to read

Present Tense:	я чита́ю ты чита́ешь он чита́ет мы чита́ем вы чита́ете они́ чита́ют
Past Tense:	чита́л (*m.*) чита́ла (*f.*) чита́ло (*n.*) чита́ли (*pl.*)
Future Tense:	я бу́ду ты бу́дешь он бу́дет мы бу́дем вы бу́дете они́ бу́дут } чита́ть

Conditional:	чита́л бы
	чита́ла бы
	чита́ло бы
	чита́ли бы
Imperative:	чита́й
	чита́йте

Participles:

Active:

Present Tense:	чита́ющий
Past Tense:	чита́вший

Passive:

Present Tense:	чита́емый

Gerund:

Present Tense:	чита́я

SECOND CONJUGATION

говори́ть to speak

Present Tense:	я говорю́
	ты говори́шь
	он говори́т
	мы говори́м
	вы говори́те
	они́ говоря́т
Past Tense:	говори́л (*m.*)
	говори́ла (*f.*)
	говори́ло (*n.*)
	говори́ли (*pl.*)

Future Tense:	я бу́ду ты бу́дешь он бу́дет мы бу́дем вы бу́дете они́ бу́дут	говори́ть

Conditional:

говори́л бы
говори́ла бы
говори́ло бы
говори́ли бы

Imperative:

говори́
говори́те

Participles:

Present Tense: говоря́щий
Past Tense: говори́вший

Gerund:

Present Tense: говоря́

B. Mixed Conjugation—Present Tense

хоте́ть TO WANT	
я хочу́ ты хо́чешь он хо́чет	мы хоти́м вы хоти́те они́ хотя́т

NOTE
This verb in the singular has first conjugation endings, with the т changing to ч. In the plural it has second-conjugation endings. The past tense is regular.

C. Reflexive Verbs:

Verbs ending with -ся or -сь are reflexive (-ся usually follows a consonant, and -сь a vowel). These verbs follow the general form of conjugation, retaining the endings -ся after consonants and -сь after vowels.

занима́ться TO STUDY	
я занима́юсь ты занима́ешься он занима́ется	мы занима́емся вы занима́етесь они́ занима́ются

D. The Verb "To Be"

The verb "to be" (быть) is usually omitted in the present tense, but is used in the past tense:

был (*m.*)
была́ (*f.*)
бы́ло (*n.*)
бы́ли (*pl.*)

and in the future tense:

я бу́ду	мы бу́дем
ты бу́дешь	вы бу́дете
он бу́дет	они́ бу́дут

It is also used as an auxiliary verb in the imperfective future.

E. Conjugations of Some Irregular Verbs in the Present Tense

БРАТЬ TO TAKE	
я беру́	мы берём
ты берёшь	вы берёте
он берёт	они́ беру́т

ВЕСТИ́ TO LEAD	
я веду́	мы ведём
ты ведёшь	вы ведёте
он ведёт	они́ веду́т

ЖИТЬ TO LIVE	
я живу́	мы живём
ты живёшь	вы живёте
он живёт	они́ живу́т

ЗВАТЬ TO CALL	
я зову́	мы зовём
ты зовёшь	вы зовёте
он зовёт	они́ зову́т

НЕСТИ́ TO CARRY	
я несу́	мы несём
ты несёшь	вы несёте
он несёт	они́ несу́т

ДАВА́ТЬ TO GIVE	
я даю́	мы даём
ты даёшь	вы даёте
он даёт	они́ даю́т

F. Conjugations of Irregular Perfective Verbs—Perfective Future

ДАТЬ TO GIVE	
я дам	мы дади́м
ты дашь	вы дади́те
он даст	они́ даду́т

СЕСТЬ TO SIT DOWN	
я ся́ду	мы ся́дем
ты ся́дешь	вы ся́дете
он ся́дет	они́ ся́дут

G. Perfective and Imperfective Aspects of a Verb

Russian verbs can be perfective or imperfective. Imperfective verbs express continuous action. They have three tenses: past, present, and future. Perfective verbs indicate completion of action, beginning of action, or both, and have only two tenses: past and future.

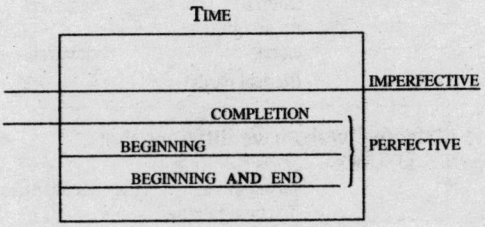

Some perfective verbs are formed by adding the prefixes с, на, вы, в, по, etc., to imperfective verbs. When a prefix is added to a verb, not only is the perfective formed, but very often the meaning of the verb is changed at the same time.

IMPERFECTIVE	PERFECTIVE
писа́ть to write	написа́ть to write down, to finish writing
	переписа́ть to copy

When the meaning of the verb changes, the new verb переписа́ть (to copy) that has been formed must have its own imperfective. To form the imperfective of such new forms, the suffix -ыв, -ив, or -ав is added:

IMPERFECTIVE	PERFECTIVE	IMPERFECTIVE
писа́ть (to write)	переписа́ть (to copy)	переписывать
чита́ть (to read)	прочита́ть (to finish reading or to read through)	прочи́тывать
	перечита́ть (to read over)	перечи́тывать
знать (to know)	узна́ть (to find out or to recognize)	узнава́ть
дава́ть (to give)	дать	
	отда́ть (to give out or away)	отдава́ть
	переда́ть (to pass)	передава́ть
	зада́ть (to assign)	задава́ть
	сдать (to deal cards)	сдава́ть

Some perfective verbs have different roots:

говори́ть (to speak)	сказа́ть (to tell)	
	заговори́ть (to begin talking)	загова́ривать

рассказа́ть (to tell a story)	расска́зывать
заказа́ть (to order something to be made or done)	зака́зывать
приказа́ть (to order, to command)	прика́зывать

Prefixes can be added to either говори́ть or сказа́ть, but each addition makes a new verb; e.g.:

за-говори́ть	to begin talking
за-каза́ть	to order something
от-говори́ть (от-гова́ривать)	to talk someone out of something
рассказа́ть	to tell a story

The past tense of the perfective verb is formed in the same way as the past tense of the imperfective verb.

H. Future Tense

The future tense has two forms: imperfective future and perfective future. As has already been pointed out, the imperfective future is formed by using the auxiliary verb быть, with the infinitive of the imperfective verb:

я бу́ду		I will	
ты бу́дешь		you will	
он бу́дет	говори́ть, чита́ть,	he will	speak, read,
мы бу́дем	понима́ть, etc.	we will	understand, etc.
вы бу́дете		you will	
они́ бу́дут		they will	

The perfective future is formed without using the auxiliary verb быть:

Present		Perfective Future	
Я пишу́	I write	я напишу́	I will write
ты говори́шь	you speak	ты ска́жешь	you will say
он идёт	he goes	он придёт	he will come
мы чита́ем	we read	мы прочита́ем	we will read (it)

Present		Perfective Future	
вы смо́трите	you look	вы посмо́трите	you will look
они́ е́дут	they go [ride]	они́ прие́дут	they will come [riding]

NOTE
The perfective verb is conjugated in the same way as the imperfective verb.

I. Verbs of Motion

Verbs of motion have many variations of meaning. A different verb is used to express movement by a conveyance than is used to express movement by foot.

Each of these verbs (i.e., indicating movement by foot or movement by conveyance) has two forms: one describes a single action in one direction, and the other, a repeated action. All of these forms are imperfective. The perfective is formed by adding a prefix to a single-action verb. But bear in mind that the addition of the prefix changes the meaning of the verb. The same prefix affixed to the repeated-action verb forms the imperfective of the new verb.

IMPERFECTIVE	REPEATED ACTION		ONE ACTION	PERFECTIVE
	ходи́ть	to go on foot	идти́	
	е́здить	to go by vehicle	е́хать	
выходи́ть		to go out on foot		вы́йти
выезжа́ть		to go out by vehicle		вы́ехать
приходи́ть		to come on foot [arrive]		прийти́
приезжа́ть		to come by vehicle [arrive]		прие́хать
заходи́ть		to drop in [visit] on foot		зайти́
заезжа́ть		to drop in [visit] by vehicle		зае́хать
	носи́ть	to carry on foot	нести́	
	вози́ть	to carry by vehicle	везти́	
приноси́ть		to bring on foot		принести́
привози́ть		to bring by vehicle		привезти́

ИДТИ́ TO GO ON FOOT (SINGLE ACTION IN ONE DIRECTION)	
PRESENT TENSE	PAST TENSE
я иду́ ты идёшь он идёт мы идём вы идёте они́ иду́т	он шёл она́ шла оно́ шло они́ шли

ХОДИ́ТЬ TO GO ON FOOT (REPEATED ACTION)	
PRESENT TENSE	PAST TENSE
я хожу́ ты хо́дишь он хо́дит мы хо́дим вы хо́дите они́ хо́дят	Regular

É́ХАТЬ TO GO BY VEHICLE (SINGLE ACTION IN ONE DIRECTION)	
PRESENT TENSE	PAST TENSE
я е́ду ты е́дешь он е́дет мы е́дем вы е́дете они́ е́дут	Regular

éздить TO GO BY VEHICLE (REPEATED ACTION)	
PRESENT TENSE	PAST TENSE
я éзжу ты éздишь он éздит мы éздим вы éздите они́ éздят	Regular

НЕСТИ́ TO CARRY ON FOOT (SINGLE ACTION IN ONE DIRECTION)	
PRESENT TENSE	PAST TENSE
я несу́ ты несёшь он несёт мы несём вы несёте они́ несу́т	 он нёс она́ несла́ оно́ несло́ они́ несли́

НОСИ́ТЬ TO CARRY ON FOOT (REPEATED ACTION)	
PRESENT TENSE	PAST TENSE
я ношу́ ты но́сишь он но́сит мы но́сим вы но́сите они́ но́сят	Regular

ВЕЗТИ́ TO CARRY BY VEHICLE (SINGLE ACTION IN ONE DIRECTION)	
PRESENT TENSE	PAST TENSE
я везу́ ты везёшь он везёт мы везём вы везёте они́ везу́т	он вёз она́ везла́ оно́ везло́ они́ везли́

ВОЗИ́ТЬ TO CARRY BY VEHICLE (REPEATED ACTION)	
PRESENT TENSE	PAST TENSE
я вожу́ ты во́зишь он во́зит мы во́зим вы во́зите они́ во́зят	Regular

J. SUBJUNCTIVE AND CONDITIONAL MOODS

The subjunctive and conditional in many languages constitute one of the most difficult grammatical constructions. However, in Russian they are the easiest. To form the subjunctive or conditional, the past tense of the verb is used together with the particle бы:

е́сли бы	if
Е́сли бы я знал }	If I knew, Had I known,

Я пошёл бы.	I would have gone. I would go.
Я позвони́л бы, е́сли бы у меня́ был ваш но́мер.	I would have called you, if I had your telephone number.

K. Imperative Mood

The imperative mood of a verb (see page 171) is formed from the second-person singular, present tense. For the singular imperative, replace the ending with -и, -й, or -ь. For the plural imperative, add -те to the singular:

Infinitive	Second-Person Singular	Familiar, Singular	Polite, Plural
писа́ть to write	пи́ш-ешь	пиши́!	пиши́те!
повторя́ть to repeat	повторя́-ешь	повторя́й!	повторя́йте!
броса́ть to throw	броса́-ешь	броса́й!	броса́йте!
рабо́тать to work	рабо́та-ешь	рабо́тай!	рабо́тайте!
чита́ть to read	чита́-ешь	чита́й!	чита́йте!

The reflexive verb retains its endings (-ся after a consonant or -й, and -сь after a vowel):

мы́ться to wash (oneself)	мо́-ешься	мо́йся!	мо́йтесь!
занима́ться to study	занима́ешься	занима́йся!	занима́йтесь!

In giving an order indirectly to a third person, the forms пусть and пускáй are used with the third person singular:

Пусть он читáет.	Let him read.	(He should read.)
Пускáй онá говорúт.	Let her speak.	(She should speak.)

L. Participles and Gerunds

Participles and gerunds are very important parts of the Russian language, so it is necessary to know how to recognize them and to understand them. However, it should be made clear that they are not used very much in simple conversation, but rather in literature and scientific writing.

Participles are verb-adjectives; gerunds are verb-adverbs. Participles are adjectives made out of verbs. The difference between an adjective and a participle is that a participle retains the verbal qualities of tense, aspect and voice. In every other respect they are adjectives. They have three genders: masculine, feminine, and neuter. They decline the same as adjectives and agree with the words they modify in gender, case, and number.

	Present	Past
Говорúть	говорящий, -ая, -ее, -ие	говорúвший, -ая, -ее, -ие

PREPOSITIONAL PLURAL:

Мы говорúм о говорящих по-англúйски ученикáх.
We are talking about students who speak English.

Gerunds are verb-adverbs and as such do not change, but have present and past tense. The present tense is formed from the imperfective; the past tense must be formed from the perfective. The present tense is characterized by two actions that take place at the same time. In the past tense, one action follows the other; when the first action is completed, the second one starts.

Present tense:

чита́ть	Чита́я, он улыба́лся. While reading, he was smiling (two simultaneous actions).

Past tense:

прочита́ть	Прочита́в газе́ту, он встал и ушёл. Having finished reading the paper, he got up and went away (one action following the other).

LETTER WRITING

A. A Note on Letter Writing

Both in formal and informal writing, the addressee's name, title, and postal address usually appear only on the envelope. In formal letters, an institution's name and address often appear at the top of the document, while the date is found at the bottom of the page.

Since the demise of the Soviet Union, the form of address in formal writing has changed. Instead of writing to a "comrade" (това́рищ), Russians now write to Mr. or Mrs. (господи́н, госпожа́). The abbreviated forms are г-н (or simply г.) for Mr. and г-жа for Mrs. In formal writing the use of a title is common, and if one wants to write to editorial offices of newspapers or journals, the phrase "Dear editorial board" (Уважа́емая реда́кция) is commonly used.

The abbreviated form of the date differs from the one used in the United States. December 20, 1992, for example, is written as 20-12-92 or as 20/XII/92. Address writing is different as well. Russians begin with the city, then write the street and house number, then apartment number, then the name of the addressee (in dative case).

B. Business Letters

г. Москва 157332
Ул. Петрова, д. 8
Всероссийское издательство «Наука»
Отдел по международным связям

Уважаемый г. Степанов!

Мы получили Ваш заказ на доставку последних номеров журнала «Континент». К сожалению, в связи с повышением почтовых тарифов, мы не смогли отправить заказ вовремя. Доставка журналов ожидается в первых числах ноября.

С уважением,
Г. И. Аполлонов
Директор отдела по
международным связям

12 октября 2002
г. Москва

Moskva 157332
Petrova 8
All-Russian Publishing House "Science"
Section on Foreign Affairs

Dear Mr. Stepanov,

We have received your order to deliver the latest issues of the journal *Kontinent*. Unfortunately, due to the increases in postal tariffs, we could not send you your order on time. The delivery of the issues is expected in early November.

Sincerely,
G. I. Apollonov
Director of the Section on
Foreign Affairs

October 12, 2002
Moscow

г. Москва 122771
Ул. Васнецова, д. 2
Совместное предприятие «Роза»

Уважаемый г. Кожинов!

Отвечаем на Ваш запрос о возможности установить торговые связи с Германией. К сожалению, в настоящее время мы не в состоянии помочь Вам в этом деле. Наше предприятие не уполномочено действовать в качестве посредника между западными и русскими фирмами.

С уважением,
Н. И. Сошников
Директор предприятия

13/XI/02
г. Москва

Moskva 122771
Vasnetsova St. 2
Joint Venture "Rose"

Dear Mr. Kozhinov,

This is in response to your inquiry about the possibility of establishing trade contacts with Germany. Unfortunately, we are unable to help you at present. Our business is not authorized to act as mediators between Western and Russian firms.

Sincerely,
N. I. Soshnikov
Director of the firm

November 13, 2002
Moscow

C. Informal Letters

27-10-02

Дорогой Иван!

Наконец, приехал в Псков. С билетами было трудно, но, в конце концов, Ирина достала и даже на скорый поезд. В общем, могу взяться за работу. Директор нашёл неплохую квартиру. Наверное, действитедьно хотят, чтобы мне было удобно. Жалко, что не успели поговорить в Москве, но в ноябре собираюсь приехать и, конечно, позвоню.

Скучаю по московским друзьям. Не забывай. Пиши!

Твой Сергей

10-27-02

Dear Ivan,

I have finally arrived in Pskov. There was difficulty with the tickets, but in the end Irina managed to get them and even for an express train. So, I can get down to work. The director found a decent apartment. It seems they really want to make me comfortable. Too bad we didn't have time to talk in Moscow, but I plan to come in November and will call you of course.

I miss my Moscow friends. Don't forget me. Write!

Your Sergei

17-11-02

Дорогая Наташа!

Давно уже не получаю от тебя писем и очень беспокоюсь о родителях. Как здоровье отца? Собирается мама уходить на пенсию или опять откладывает? Позвони мне на работу, домашний телефон ещё не подключили.
Девочки растут, Марина пошла в первый класс и очень гордится. Таня даёт ей советы.
Все у нас хорошо. Миша передаёт привет. Надеюсь увидеть всех вас на праздники.

Целую,
Ваша Галя

11-17-02

Dear Natasha,

I have not received letters from you in a while and I worry a lot about our parents. How is Father's health? Is Mom going to retire or is she delaying again? Call me at work: our home phone has not yet been connected.
The girls are growing. Marina started first grade and is very proud. Tania gives her advice.
Everything is fine with us. Misha sends regards. I hope to see all of you for the holidays.

Kisses,
Your Galia

D. Form of the Envelope

1. Business Letters

г. Москва 332889
ул. Страхова, д.5, кв.75
Павлову Ивану Петровичу

г. Псков 32435
ул. Надеждина, д.4,кв. 11
Сергей Суриков

Moscow 332889
Strakhova St. 5, apt.75
Pavlov, Ivan Petrovich

Pskov 32435
Nadezhdina St. 4, apt. 11
Sergei Surikov

2. Informal Letters

г. Ставрополь 32456
ул. Кураева, д.1, кв.75
Семеновой Наталье Ивановне

г. Новосибирск 30897
ул. Королёва, д.15, кв. 33
Г.И. Синицына

Stavropol 32456
Kuraeva 1, apt.75
Semenova Natalia Ivanovna

Novosibirsk 30897
Koroleva 15, apt.33
Sinitsina G.I.

Also available from **LIVING LANGUAGE®**

ULTIMATE RUSSIAN

Beginner-Intermediate or Advanced

Equivalent to two years of college-level study, this comprehensive program covers reading, writing, grammar, conversation, and culture. Includes a coursebook and eight 60-minute CDs.

Beginner-Intermediate
CD/Coursebook Program • 1-4000-2117-0 • $79.95/C$110.00
Coursebook only • 1-4000-2116-2 • $18.00/C$26.00

Advanced
CD/Coursebook Program • 1-4000-2072-7 • $79.95/C$120.00
Coursebook only • 1-4000-2070-0 • $18.00/C$27.00

IN-FLIGHT RUSSIAN

Wondering how to make use of all that spare time on the plane while you're flying to Moscow or St. Petersburg? Between your in-flight meal and in-flight movie, brush up on your Russian! This 60-minute program covers just enough to get by in every travel situation.

0-609-81077-4 • $13.95/C$21.00